Tales From A Singer-Songwriter

Volume One: A Spiritual Road

By
Randi Perkins

AMERISONG
NASHVILLE, TENNESSEE

©2009 by AmeriSong, Inc.
5401 Wakefield Dr, Nashville TN 37220

All Rights Reserved. No part of this document may be reproduced in any form or by any means without written permission from the publisher

Cover photo & cover design: Wayne Hall

Back cover photo: Clark Perkins

Edited by: Clark Perkins

Printed in the United States of America

Library of Congress Cataloging-in-Publication Data

Perkins, Randi C, 1952-
Title: Tales From A Singer-Songwriter, Volume One: A Spiritual Road

ISBN   978-0-578-03102-6

www.amerisong.com
www.randiperkins.com

This is a collection of real life stories for all people out there seeking a path to their destiny…… in all walks of life.

Life is a Spiritual Road……a journey that transcends all religions, institutions, and governments and brings us home to our roots and the soul within us.

If you can see it, and you can believe it……the passion in your soul will reveal the road to get there.

Table of Contents

Acknowledgements   7

Introduction   8

Who Is Randi Perkins?   10

Singer-Songwriter, A Definition   12

Chapter:
1. Counting My Blessings   15
2. Of Elementary Music and Grace   18
3. Most Avid Ballplayer   20
4. Young Imagination-The Band, On The Road As A Teenager   24
5. Who Ran Over The Damn Trees?   30
6. The Tornado   33
7. Doug Kershaw, Chance Encounter   36
8. A Special Meeting with Kris Kristofferson   38
9. Ronnie Milsap and the Power of Music   41
10. Bowling and the Music Business   44
11. Larry Hogoboom, Not Your Ordinary Friend   48
12. My Dear Friend And First Producer, Mike Crowley   54
13. Oh, Brother…Learning Life While Spinning Out of Control   58
14. About The Song *"When I Think I'm Gonna Fall In Love"*   62
15. *"The Last Harvest"*, The Story Behind The Song   65
16. 2nd Graders Dig Singer-Songwriters Too!   69

17. Jock Bartley from FireFall, a Regular Guy   71
18. You're Just Gonna Have To Deal With Aubrey Collins
                                                              73
19. Randi…Please Stand Up!   76
20. 1200 Miles Without Radio…Searching   80
21. The Second Coming of Mark Nelson   83
22. Grandma Benson's Piano   89
23. A Story Of Guitars And Spirits   93
24. Of Buzzards and Hugh Bennett   97

The Mountain (A Poem)   100

Continuing The Journey   102

Acknowledgements

I am blessed to have a wonderful family who has shared this road with me in one way or another. My wife, Sandy, and my son, Clark. My Dad, Robert W (Bud) Perkins, and my Mom, Myrtice A Perkins. My brother, Mark, and my sister, Julie, and of course, my late brother, Scott.

My dear childhood friends, Marvin Brown and Curtis Johnson, we grew up together and will always share that special bond. Friends brought close by fate along the way, Larry Hogoboom, Garth Shaw, and the Taylors... Jerry, Janet and Abby. Wendy Vickers, for the encouragement. Dave Pelton for the time and insight. Larry Richardson for spiritual insight.

Artists who have allowed me the pleasure of being part of their careers, Kathy and Kelly Perkins (my nieces), Aubrey Collins, and Kelly Aspen.

Scott's daughter, Chelsea Perkins Moser, for giving me some valued marketing input, and all of my other nieces, nephews, and in-laws.

Glen Wolf, Clark Talkington, and Grace Brittner, my music teachers, where a vital part of this music in me all began. My music friends from the old days at Dickinson State.

Music industry folks who have shared time and knowledge with me, Tim Dubois, Kyle Lehning, Rod Essig, Rod Harris, Butch Baker, Jay Orr, Hugh Bennett, Cathy Lemmon, J Gary Smith, Johnny Morris...all have allowed me vital insight for my musical journey.

Introduction

Life is a journey, a long road with a lot of experiences, the good, the bad, and the learning that results from them. It's all just part of a story. These stories represent a celebration of life.

I am driven and passionate about my life as a singer-songwriter and feel called to share the tales of the journey so that people may relate them to their own life and careers.

The more time goes by, the more I become convinced that we are born with a calling in life. We may have a duty and responsibility to seek out that calling. This is a challenging road for which there are many obscure signs and deceiving twists and turns.

Following the road requires much inward reflection and staying in touch with our instincts. We usually have feelings that draw us in a particular direction for which we may not understand. Quite often, this direction may defy our accepted sense of reality. Does anyone know what it feels like to make decisions because of money? Of course, this is the common factor that we rationalize with all of the time and will continually pull us from our path. It can be a very fine line to make decisions based on what our hearts tell us versus what we rationalize because of money or any similar distraction.

If we accept the notion that we were born with a calling, then making a decision that pulls us away from that calling is a betrayal of our being. It really is a betrayal of our sense of right and wrong. In my case, I believe God bestowed this individual calling upon me, and if I betray this calling, I am betraying God. In fact, other people's lives may depend upon our fulfilling the call that we have received. People in these stories I have written, made choices that resulted in their being in my life.

In this book, I am relating the stories of my experiences that have served to give me a better picture of my own calling. I may never see the entire picture or may never know whose life may have depended on me, but I am driven to move forward with keener senses in the hope that I will recognize the best choices when they need to be made. I think that on this road of life, the signs are visible if we are prepared to see them. Our experiences make these signs more visible and the road becomes clearer.

Sometimes the strangest of things happen, things that cannot be explained by a means other than divine intervention. I have had a few of those. Looking back, I can only surmise that these are the signs. I want to encourage everyone to take a look at their own experiences in life, past and present, and to interpret how these experiences may relate to their own calling.

I say that I am a singer-songwriter. Actually, I think it is more appropriate to say that I am an observer and interpreter of life with the purpose of relating my experiences so that others may benefit and live a better life because of an experience I have written about that touches them. And who knows, it may inspire someone to seek out their calling.

Randi Perkins

Who Is Randi Perkins?

Singer-Songwriter Randi Perkins was influenced by the likes of Dan Fogelberg, Gordon Lightfoot, Jim Croce and John Denver. His music reflects a broad spectrum of life experience and being passionate about the legacy of singer-songwriters, he has been quoted as saying his mission is to "bring the singer-songwriter spirit back to the heart of America." John Denver, who was a close friend of Randi's first producer, once called Randi a "very gifted poetic songwriter."

Randi grew up on a farm near a small town called Scranton in Southwestern North Dakota, and in early years, attended a one room schoolhouse. Ever since he realized people actually created songs, he wanted to be a songwriter and began writing songs when he was 17. A performer at an early age, learning guitar helped him to bring his songs to audiences. Before settling in to his folk singer-songwriter roots, Randi graduated from Dickinson State University in Dickinson, North Dakota where he majored in music and business and he participated in nationally acclaimed music groups including jazz band, choir, and symphonic band. He currently lives in Nashville, Tennessee with his wife, Sandy & his son, Clark.

Prior to college days, Randi was a founder and songwriter in the 1970's influential rock band, *Young Imagination*, who captured the attention of many folks in the upper Great Plains. *Young Imagination* recorded at Sound 80 Studios in Minneapolis and released a record that received notable radio airplay in the region. Randi was honored to have his song *"Dakota, I've Not Forgotten"* chosen to represent North Dakota's Centennial Celebration in 1989 which earned him numerous radio and TV interviews and concert appearances. He performed on CBS TV with Roy Clark and Bobby Vee during the course of the Centennial Celebration. He was a male vocalist winner in the Country Western Jamboree in Dickinson, and was a winner in a True Value/Jimmy Dean Country Showdown contest in 1996 with his nieces and brother.

As a songwriter with depth in his music and lyrics, Randi was a finalist in the coveted 1974 American Song Festival out of 60,000 entries and has been a winner in a number of song competitions including the NSAI/CMT Songwriting Competition and the USA Songwriting Competition.

Discography

2008 *"Life Is Good"*

2000 *"The Songwriter"*

1989 *"Dakota Dream"*

Published Author – In addition to *Tales From A Singer-Songwriter*, Randi is also a co-author of article on music business in *Mix Magazine*, and co-authored a text used in the music business program at University of Colorado / Denver and is a contributing author on *Navigating The Music Business* by Dick Weissman and Frank Jermance published by Hal Leonard Publishing.

Teaching - Part-time faculty 1995–1998 at the University of Colorado/Denver teaching *Music Industry Financial Management*. Randi is also a CPA and an MBA

Artist Development - Randi has been instrumental in the careers of Kelly Aspen, Kat Perkins, and Aubrey Collins who was the lead singer for the country band, *Trick Pony* for most of 2007.

Singer-Songwriter, A Definition

As a singer-songwriter, I draw upon my roots, my family, my friends, my experiences, my observations, and my instincts and seek to relate them to others in a personal delivery of the songs through performance and recording.

Living in Nashville, I am amongst hundreds of others who refer to themselves as "singer-songwriters" and I have come to realize that we are not all the same. In fact, I believe that I belong to a special class of artists, relating personal experiences through song in my own way. I draw upon the influence of the 70's singer-songwriters such as Dan Fogelberg, Gordon Lightfoot, James Taylor, Billy Joel and John Denver.

Over the years, many people have come to Nashville with big dreams of being successful songwriters, lured by thoughts of fame and money. A whole industry has grown up around teaching, coaching, and critiquing songwriting and attempting to impose certain rules upon the craft. Even though I believe that a certain amount of songwriting can be taught and I admit we are all learning and growing in the craft, the true seed of songwriting comes from the soul. People like me are born into it and are destined to follow the calling.

Songwriting attracts many different kinds of people for different reasons, most of the time it is the perceived lifestyle, fame, money, the process, or the kind of people. The Nashville publishing community and the need for relationships has proliferated the idea of "co-writing," which has largely expanded the definition of "songwriter." It is widely perceived that basically anyone could be a "songwriter." I would agree that anyone who is passionate about something can achieve it, but maybe there should be some distinctions in the definition of "songwriter" and the components that make up the process.

In a recent Nashville newspaper article about a pro football quarterback who writes "songs" and is setting up a publishing company, the "songwriter" commented that he was sometimes intimidated because he wasn't very "musical". A well-known songwriter and recording artist responded that "you don't have to be musical to write songs." Now, if you are not musical, I think your contribution to a song is as a "lyricist" or "song idea person" and you are not really a "songwriter."

In the Nashville social scene, the first question that comes up is "do you want to get together and write." For political and economical reasons, it is perceived by most in the songwriting and publishing community that "co-writing" is the primary means to success in Nashville. If one only contributes to songs through collaboration, then you are a co-songwriter or "co-writer" and not really a songwriter in the true sense of the word. I am not being critical of "co-writing" because it is valuable tool for some people and I have done some "co-writing" myself, but my co-writing is an activity outside of what I do as a singer-songwriter.

One of the ways to get exposure to the Nashville community is through participating in writer's nights where a group of songwriters get up on stage and take turns performing their songs. Writer's nights are a great way to hone your performing skills and meet other songwriters. Most of these performers would refer to themselves as singer-songwriters, but in reality, they are usually "co-writers who sing." This may not seem like an important distinction to some, but to a singer-songwriter artist like me, the ability to sing and co-write songs does not necessarily make one a "singer-songwriter."

We all need to seek our paths to success in our own ways. "Success" in the songwriting business may take many forms and many meanings. It may be defined as a level of commercial success or it may be something else. There are places for everyone who can lend their talents to the components that make up a song and each can attain their own definition of success. For me, success would be fulfilling my destiny through relating my life experiences in songs delivered through my own personal performance and making a difference in someone's life.

If I write a song with someone else, I am a "co-writer." If I sing a song I didn't write, I am a "singer". If I perform a song that I co-wrote, I am a singer/co-writer. But the thing that really drives me is the pursuit of my soul's passion to relate my own ideas in my own way as an artist. I am a singer-songwriter.

Chapter One

Counting My Blessings

I received an email from a friend of mine who, like many of us, moved to Nashville a number of years ago to write songs and to find commercial success as a songwriter. She expressed that she has gotten caught up in her day to day life, trying to make a living, and her songwriting goals are slipping away. She was looking for advice/assistance on playing guitar and becoming more self sufficient as to not rely so much on other writers for the music and melodies. Basically, she was a lyric writer only. Her words expressed the passion and desire of attaining success as a songwriter which is the necessary element and prerequisite found in the ones who do succeed.

I understood her perfectly, because I too have that passion and desire. She made me aware of how important it is for the ones of us with like passions to support one another as best we can. She also made me reflect on my own experience in the music industry and count my blessings. It is very easy to get down on oneself here in Nashville and think "why can't I be a better singer or guitar player or performer," "I have this talent and passion and I just need more tools to make it happen," or "Why don't I have what that person has."

Well, now I realize that my friend with her passion and desire can make it work. She needs a little help like we all do, but all things are possible. With this realization, I need to count my blessings.

Why am I counting my blessings? Because now when I don't feel I have attained the level of success that I expected, I realize there are many who have attained success with far less tools and experience than I have. I have written songs... lyrics AND melodies AND music, for many years. I was, for a time, a music major in college studying performance, music theory and arranging. I can play guitar AND keyboard reasonably well. I have performed in a band AND solo and sometimes in front of thousands of people. I have performed live on TV and been on TV and radio talk shows. I have heard my songs on the radio and heard my songs performed by other artists. I have recorded three albums that I am proud of. I have had publishers sign my songs and have been a winner in multiple song contests. And in addition, I have successfully managed artists, written books, and taught music business in college.

Will I ever be in a singer-songwriters hall of fame? I don't know, but if not, it won't be because I don't have the ability to do it. I believe the greatest gift that God gave me is the passion and desire to attain success as a singer-songwriter, not the singing or performing talent. Many people with passion like me have risen to the top with much less than I have. I can't make excuses for any lack of success, I can only work towards my goal every day and use the tools I was given to the best of my ability and enjoy the process. It's my calling and it's what God expects me to do.

I also had this other life as a CPA/MBA with tons of business experience. That too is a tool I have, however, my first few years in Nashville have been caught up in trying to make a living on the business side of the music industry in order to create opportunities for me as a singer-songwriter. That concept has never worked; I have learned that lesson over and over. A few months ago, another close friend of mine in the music community told me that I could never really be happy or successful "running alongside my dream." Well, now that makes sense to me. I AM A SINGER-SONGWRITER, for better or for worse, it's what I do, it's my life. All of the people around me will benefit from my facing up to that reality. I must have faith that God will provide the necessary relationships and resources to make my success possible.

Maybe the greatest blessing I have received is that I have recognized my calling in this life, because I'm sure many people never do.

Chapter Two

Of Elementary Music And Grace

The fifth grade was sort of a pivotal year for me. I had just been coaxed into starting beginning band by my Mom, which I first resisted, thinking it may cause me to not be accepted in my peer group. If I was in the "band," especially playing saxophone, it may force me further from acceptance which I dearly sought. But, I did join and later switched to trumpet, and I now know that joining the school band proved to be one of the most gratifying experiences I ever had. Looking back, I know that I was always destined to be different from my peers and that those differences needed to be cherished and celebrated. Truth is, we are all different from our peers in some way.

In addition to band, we had an elementary music teacher named Grace Brittner. Grace was the seventh grade teacher, but she also taught general music and singing to our fifth grade class every week. The first time she taught our class, she walked around the room and asked each one of us if we liked music and singing, and encouraged all of us to talk about it to the class. Grace and her family were close friends with my Mom's family. Her daughter used to live at my Grandparent's house in Bowman, North Dakota while she was attending high school there. So consequently, Grace knew a lot about my Mom's background.

In that first music class, Grace made her way around the room, and when she finally got to me, her face lit up as she asked me if I was a good singer. She said "I have known your mother a long time, and I used to enjoy listening to her and her sisters sing at community events", "Since your mother is a good singer, you must be a good singer also". Now, I was pretty much a shy and reserved kid, and at this point was kind of shrinking into my seat. It got worse; Grace asked if I would get up and sing in front of the class.

At this point in my life, I don't think I had sung for anyone... alone, except at home, maybe singing along with a TV commercial or something. However, Grace kept after me, she said "I know that you know The Star-Spangled Banner, why don't you sing that for us?" To this day, I don't know what came over me at that moment, maybe it was the "Grace" of God or something. I got up in front of the class and sang "The Star-Spangled Banner."

When I went home after school that day and told my Mom about singing in music class because of Grace, she was very proud of me. I'm sure she was also a little flattered that Grace had commented on "The Benson Sisters" vocal talents in front of my class.

The following week when Grace walked into music class, she asked if anyone had any suggestions for what they would like to do in class that day. To my surprise, a group of girls raised their hands and said "we want to hear Randi sing The Star-Spangled Banner again." Grace granted their request and I sang it again. I'm sure a few of my male classmates were jealous and I don't think it helped me fit in any easier, either. But at that moment, it didn't matter.

I will be ever grateful to Grace Brittner for that moment. It took my self-confidence up many notches. It was that "perfect storm" of school band, elementary music, and the thought that some girls actually wanted to hear me sing, that brought me to the world of music I live in today.

Chapter Three

Most Avid Ballplayer

In 1961, Minneapolis, Minnesota got a new major league baseball team, the Twins. The games were usually broadcast on the local TV station (the only one we could get) and my family and I became big fans of the Twins. Like many of the other kids in town, I wanted to play baseball. My folks finally bought me a baseball glove from the Sears & Roebuck catalog and I was itching to get out and break it in. This actually began a long trend of acquiring baseball accessories and Twins memorabilia including the collecting of baseball cards. My life became obsessed with playing and being a fan of baseball.

My Dad would play catch with me and I started to learn to use my new glove. One day in the spring of 1963, we went to Scranton for a Babe Ruth League baseball game. I realized that a couple of the kids playing were my age. I inquired about joining the team and was told to ask the coach, Louis Getz. I found out that it was OK, so I joined. Most of the kids were a lot older, and even though we got to dress for the games, I wasn't hopeful about playing.

As luck would have it, my uncle, David Leer, in Bismarck was also big fan of baseball and he had played quite a lot and knew how to pitch. He taught me how to throw a curve ball. I was inspired and went back to the farm and set up an old bedspring against the wall of an old garage and started practicing my pitching. Before long, I had developed the meanest curveball on the Scranton team, even at my young age. In addition, my Dad had built a homemade "tee" to hold the ball while I practiced hitting.

Even though I didn't initially get to play in the games with the Scranton team, I went to all of the practices and made the most of all the possible opportunities to bat, throw, and catch. It seems I would get up every morning and practice pitching and batting all day out on the farm in addition to going to practice with the team. I was getting pretty confident and knew that my skills were starting to equal some of the older kids, and I was much better than the kids my age.

Louis Getz, the coach, began to pay attention. He eventually put me in some games, starting in right field, the usual spot for beginners. But Louis knew I worked hard and he rewarded me with some playing time in the infield. As I became more confident, I told him I could pitch. One day, in a game against a team that was not as good as we were, Louis let me pitch the first 2 innings. I was snapping off that curve ball like a pro and threw it almost every pitch. The batters would back out of the box and the ball would go right over the plate! The only trouble was, I was only about 4' 10" tall and could not throw a fastball very hard. It would be the only time I would pitch that year but, nonetheless, Louis took notice.

Towards the end of the season, we were playing a game against Hettinger and were short handed, so I got to play. It was a big game and the opposing pitcher was fast! I was batting ninth, and as I watched the rest of our players get up and strike out or hit the ball feebly, I got a little nervous. But, I had practiced hard all year and knew I could hit the ball if I just could hang in there. I finally stepped in the batters box and eyed the pitcher, he looked to be something just short of Goliath! The pitcher eyed me back, all four foot ten of me, and he grinned. I dug in and took a couple practice swings, and a deep breath. The pitcher wound up and I knew that pitch was coming in hard and fast right down the middle. I kept my eye on the ball and swung with all of my hopes and dreams in that moment. It was almost like the imagery of Casey's last swing in "Casey At The Bat," only to my excitement, the results were different. I hit a solid line drive over the second baseman's head into right field for a hit. I was the first batter on our team to get a hit in the game.

The next batter struck out for the third out. Before we went out on the field for the next inning, Louis sat us all down on the bench to give the team a good chewing out. I was sitting on the end. Louis said "I want all of you wimps to look down at the little guy sitting at the end of the bench, he has the only hit on this team!" Time stood still, I felt sort of embarrassed for a moment and Louis continued "If he can hit, all of you can hit". On that note, we all sprang from the bench and took the field a more determined team. When the final out was tallied, we had won the game! That would prove to be my only hit that season, but what a fine moment it was!

After the season was over, Coach Louis held an awards banquet and I attended with my Dad. With only one hit and limited playing time, I knew I wasn't in line for any of the awards but wanted to be there to support the team. Some of the players had impressive stats and I was happy for them as they proudly accepted their awards. After seemingly all of the awards had been handed out and Louis had thanked every one for a great season, he paused...... and he continued...... "I have one more award to hand out." The room became very quiet and Louis said "I am giving the award for MOST AVID BALLPLAYER to Randi Perkins." I was stunned and bewildered as I rose to accept the award. There was polite applause and I graciously thanked Louis as he put that ribbon in my hand. As we left the building and were walking to the car, I said "Dad, what does "avid" mean? He sort of gave me an explanation, but said I should look it up in the dictionary when we got home.

In the coming years, I enjoying some success at baseball as a teenager, but I realized I probably would not be cut out to be a professional baseball player. Music and songs were begging for my attention and were gnawing at my soul. Maybe someday I can get an award for "Most Avid Singer-Songwriter."

Chapter Four

Young Imagination-The Band On The Road As A Teenager

In my first year of high school, we had a new music teacher named Glen Wolf. Our previous music teacher, Clark Talkington, was a classically oriented guy who gave us a wonderful background in the classical history of music, but was not much into the emergence of pop and rock music of the day. Glen was different, in fact, he played in a dance band on trombone and bass guitar.

One of the first things Glen did was to start a jazz band at Scranton High. I was the first chair trumpet player in the new jazz band and my good friend, Marvin Brown, was the second chair trumpet player. My brother, Mark, played French horn but the jazz band didn't need a French horn so Glen took Mark under his wing and got him started on bass guitar. Lord knows, Mark could play about anything he put his mind to, he also later learned to play drums. One of the percussion players, Dave Czywczynski, took up the trap set and played drums for the jazz band. The jazz band also included a talented trombone player, Susan Torpen.

In my senior year of high school, Glen encouraged us to form a pop oriented band to play Tijuana Brass music, the then popular band lead by Herb Alpert. Our band included Marvin and I on trumpet, Susan on trombone, Mark on bass guitar and Dave on drums. After playing for a few events, we were itching to branch out and play some rock music from the top 40 charts. Of course, this would require a transformation. I had an electric guitar that I had never really learned to play, but now I had some motivation. I got a rock & roll guitar instruction book, and after learning bar chords, I was able to start playing those songs we heard on the radio. Marvin became our lead singer, and Dave's girlfriend, Linda Thompson, was also recruited to sing. In addition to trombone, Susan was an excellent keyboard player. All 6 of us could sing, and would eventually trade off singing background vocals.

Now we had a guitar, a bass, a drummer, a keyboard player, and two lead singers…..four guys and two girls. We came up with this incredibly creative name, *Four Plus Two* (imagine that). We printed up some posters and were off and running. It was interesting twist of fate that we had a female student teacher at Scranton, her name I don't remember, who happened to walk into one of our rehearsals. She had been in a band and told us we needed to better utilize our talents, we weren't all singing at that time. This talented student teacher taught us to sing all of the parts on the Mamas & Papas hit "Monday, Monday." We were all good singers and mastered the song in hurry and we were really pumped when we left that rehearsal! Our vocals would prove to set us a part from most bands in the upper Great Plains in those days, they usually only had one vocalist.

We were a hit in a couple of talent shows in the spring of 1970, but we needed real gigs, gigs where we could get paid. I took it upon myself to do a letter writing campaign and sent introduction letters to schools and to chambers of commerce in all of the towns within a hundred mile radius. We received enough response to those letters to keep us busy most weekends throughout the summer and fall of 1970, the buzz was beginning to build. On a trip home from one show in early summer in Hebron, North Dakota, we got to talking about changing the name of the band. "Four Plus Two" just didn't seem to cut it any more. My brother, Mark, knowing that we were young and imaginative, brilliantly suggested "Young Imagination," so ***Young Imagination*** it was. No "The" at the beginning and no "S" at the end (it seems that most bands back then started with "the" and had an "s" at the end), so it was a ground breaking decision. We wasted no time, as we passed through Dickinson on the way home, we stopped and had magnetic signs made for the doors of our vehicle and designed new posters.

Much to our dismay, the prized venue called Davis Barn, which was 9 miles south of Scranton, would elude us that year. The Davis Barn featured the best bands from all over the region in the sixties and seventies and always had a packed house. Our parents used to take us there on Friday nights during the summer before we could drive on our own, so after forming the band, it was our dream to play there. In the summer of 1971, we got our chance, and I believe we drew the biggest crowd in the history of the Davis Barn. Of course, we were the local sensation! The Davis Barn is now reduced to memories and no bands have played there for decades. The barn was sold and recently converted to a hunting lodge. Marvin's family held a family gathering there in the summer of 2008 and he invited me to attend. I brought my guitar and played a few tunes, Marvin even sang with me on one. I'm sure the old ghosts of the barn were rockin' along with us.

"We did a record," as Mark exclaimed at our reunion show in 1983. Making a record in those days was not as easy as it is today, and not many bands would record, or were even writing their own stuff. The closest major studio was in Minneapolis, Minnesota, and recording was expensive. I caught the songwriting bug early, for me, it seemed as easy to write songs as it was to learn them from the radio. Learning songs was complicated back then, you had to listen to the radio and have a great memory, or you could buy the record and keep dropping the needle down over and over until you got the chords and the words (we didn't have cassette players then). Marvin and Mark collaborated with me on writing songs, and eventually original songs would make up about half of our repertoire. The original songs and 4-part vocals made us unique and we knew that we needed to make a record.

We set a date for a recording session in early June of 1971 at Sound 80 Studios in Minneapolis. The preparation for the session and the shifting attitudes of the band members forced a change in the band. It became obvious that Mark, Marvin and I were a little more committed to the band than the others. Dave and Linda left the band, and Mark would play both bass and drums on the recording. Earlier, Mary DeMotte had replaced Susan on keyboards. We were now a 4-member band, me, Mark, Marvin, and Mary. We hired drummers when we toured.

The recording at Sound 80 went well, we recorded our original tunes *"Hard To Find Someone Who Cares"* and *"Your Friend"* which were pressed into a 45-RPM record. Looking back, it was an honor to have recorded at Sound 80 Studios because it became somewhat legendary. Numerous notable acts recorded there including Bob Dylan, Prince, Leo Kottke, Cat Stevens, Michael Johnson, Dave Brubeck and others. Also, digital recording was pioneered there in the 70's in a partnership with 3M Company.

In the spring of 1971, we had captured the attention of booking agent Ron Kohn of Panther Productions out of Chadron, Nebraska after playing at the Pink Panther Club in Chadron. Panther Productions later became Intermountain Entertainment and relocated to Rapid City, South Dakota. As an original band, and with a record out, we became Ron's top band. Our territory expanded from North and South Dakota to include Montana, Wyoming, and Nebraska and we toured in the summer of 1971. Ron had an established circuit of clubs that we worked.

I won't go into to many details, but as teenagers (I was the oldest at 19), we had a lot of interesting experiences. We had an old 1960 Suburban with rearranged seats pulling a U-Haul trailer and breakdowns were common, especially late at night. We picked up hitchhikers, had wandering fans follow us from town to town, and had people wanting to buy us beer and be our friends. We slept in sleeping bags in parks and only had motel rooms about every 3 days. Some of these things make me shudder today, especially since I am now the father of a teenager.

In those days, AM Radio was king and it was easier to get radio play. Panther Productions promoted some of our shows on the powerhouse station KOMA out of Oklahoma City, which would reach the mid section of the country from Mexico to Canada. As a kid growing up listening to KOMA on my little transistor radio at night, it was amazing to hear our band's name on that station.

I thought the big time was near. A major record label's promotion office in Minneapolis had shown some interest, I'm sure that another few months would have brought opportunities, but it was not to be. Marvin, Mary, and I went to Dickinson State University in the fall of 1971. Mark had turned his interest to other things. Marvin eventually moved. I got an acoustic guitar and yearned to be a solo singer-songwriter. As is pretty common with bands, we could not hold *Young Imagination* together.

The learning process, experience, and memories were invaluable. The business, the promotion, the music, and getting out on our own provided a wonderful opportunity for growth. I'm sure there are many old fans out there who rocked out at our dances and would have fond memories as well.

As of this writing, I have not given up hope of a reunion. I have been putting the bug in Mark and Marvin's ears...... I'm sure they think I'm nuts, but hey, stranger things have happened. The good old days might be yet to come.

Chapter Five

Who Ran Over The Damn Trees?

After graduating from Scranton Public high school in 1970, I enrolled in the National College of Business in Rapid City, South Dakota. Living away from home and making new friends was both scary and exciting, but due to my dedication to our band, *Young Imagination*, school seemed to be the farthest thing from my mind. I was back in North Dakota virtually every weekend or we were doing gigs on the weekend. College became a burden to me and I finally decided to drop out for the last half of the year in order to attend Dickinson State University the following fall and major in music. During that time I became very close to my brother, Mark.

Mark, who had recently turned 16, was also in the band and was the youngest member. I think it got him growing up a little earlier than he might have otherwise, had he not been playing with the band. While I had been gone to Rapid City, Mark was spreading his wings and as some might say "pushing the limits". He had access to a car, courtesy of our parents and he liked to get out and hang out with his buddies. Now, I was always a good kid and stayed out of trouble, so when Mark got into a little mischief here and there, my folks weren't quite sure how to react. Mark was a good kid too, but times were changing. At one point he acquired a fake ID, and even though he looked young, he was able to buy some beer from nearby towns where he wasn't recognized.

Sometime in early 1971, a few little recently planted trees in front of the Scranton Public School were deliberately run over by a car. In a town of less than 400 people, the incident was a big scandal and was the talk of the downtown café coffee crowd. And of course, the talk got around that Mark Perkins was the one who ran over the trees. Even though I suspected he might have been the culprit, Mark and I never discussed it. Finally the whole town was blaming him, the Sheriff even pulled him over one day and asked him to admit that he ran over the trees. Mom and Dad were devastated and I'm sure that they suspected him also but wanted to believe in the worst way that it wasn't him since he was denying the deed. As the pressure mounted, Mark and I even discussed getting away, maybe heading to California to work our way into the music business and maybe even the movie business (we had big dreams).

But all that was not to be. The pressure finally got to Mark and he admitted to me that he had in fact run over the trees, but he was sorry and embarrassed and wasn't sure what to do. He was afraid of the consequences. I told him that he probably better start by telling Mom and Dad. Maybe making the confession and by possibly replanting the trees, the whole incident could be smoothed over in time.

One night after Mark and I had driven around awhile in Scranton, Mark decided it was time to go home and tell the folks. I'm sure the ride home was a long one for Mark, I don't think he said a word all the way home. We pulled in the garage and went into the house. Mom and Dad were sitting in the family room watching the news on TV. Mark slowly worked his way around the corner and got their attention. He was sort of trembling a little and was choked up, but the words finally came. He said "Mom...Dad...I RAN OVER THE DAMN TREES. Even if they wanted to respond, they didn't get a chance to, because Mark promptly made his way downstairs and went to bed.

A new day dawned the next morning, the trees were eventually replanted, Mark never was charged, and the incident faded into the annals of Scranton, North Dakota history.

Chapter Six

The Tornado

There are not many things more powerful than a tornado, reaching down out of a dark sky and touching the prairies of the Great Plains, sometimes without warning. As a young North Dakota farm boy, I could never have envisioned seeing a tornado from the inside out. This was a very brutal reminder how important it is to count our blessings everyday, because life can be fragile, and can change in a heartbeat when you least expect it. Although a few material things were destroyed, I am thankful that we were all spared injury or death, and in looking to find a little good in everything, I am thankful for the wakeup call.

It was on the eve of the first extended tour of our rock band, *Young Imagination*, in June of 1971. We had completed our first record in Minneapolis and were ready to head out on the road. That afternoon, Marvin Brown, Mary DeMotte, and my brother Mark and I finished rehearsing in my grandparent's old garage across the driveway from my parent's house, and were loading our sound equipment into the U-Haul trailer attached to our old 1960 Suburban. The trailer was backed up to the big garage door, which was wide open and faced to the south. We could see some rain clouds approaching and were hurrying to get everything neatly in its place in the trailer.

In those days, weather forecasting was not very advanced. We were used to thunderstorms, lightning and hail, but tornados were sort of rare. I don't even remember if there was stormy weather in the forecast for that day, but in any case, we had no idea what was about to happen. What we thought would be a little rain shower didn't scare us much.

Before we could finish loading the equipment, the sky darkened, and the wind began to blow. The stormy weather was rolling in from the north, so we weren't able to see it from the garage door facing south. It started to rain…..it started to rain real hard. All of a sudden, the rain stopped, and we were in the midst of a deafening silence and eerie stillness…… but just for a moment. Then, the wind began to blow, and with every nano-second it became louder and louder until it reached a thundering roar. Time almost stood still, and I wasn't sure if the wind would ever stop. At this point, even as a shelf was falling off the wall in the back of that feeble garage, none of us could still imagine or understand was happening. Almost as quickly as it began, the roar stopped…… but then we could see it, it was a tornado.

As the tornado continued to the south from over top of us, there were wood granaries, a shed, and a chicken coop that just swayed for a moment, swirled, twisted, and flew apart and ascended into the funnel. We were still holding on to microphone stands and cords, and we stared in disbelief, as the tornado continued over the American Colloid plant and headed on south. Finally, coming to the realization of what had just occurred, I remembered that my parents and our younger brother, Scott, and sister, Julie, were in the house across the driveway.

"Is everyone OK" we heard, as the rest of my family came running from the house. As we ventured out of the garage, we could then see that the roof was missing from my parent's garage, and that part of the roof of the house had been lifted. A tree was pulled out by the roots just behind the garage where we were when the tornado went over us. A look to the south made us realize how many structures were missing or damaged, and especially, we realized how incredibly blessed we were, that no one was harmed. Later, I realized that having the big garage door open, probably prevented the tornado from building enough pressure inside that rickety garage to blow it apart. A few moments earlier, and the door would have been closed while we were rehearsing, one little twist of fate that probably saved our lives.

In the coming weeks, many truckloads of debris were gathered from the fields south of the farm, and I'm sure some of it is still there. But, that debris was only from material things that could be repaired or replaced. Splinters of wood were driven into boards, and even through a tractor tire…… signs of the awesome power that nature can bring upon us.

These traumatic experiences seem to have a way of being etched into our memories for the rest of our lives. Now, every time I hear a noisy gust of wind, I'm right back there……in the middle of that tornado……but, I am also reminded that life can change in an instant. A reminder……to treasure my days on this earth, and to do my best to live life to its fullest every day.

Chapter Seven

Doug Kershaw, A Chance Encounter

When I was a kid, we never traveled much or too far, and I never had flown in an airplane. In the summer of 1971, my friend, Curtis Johnson, who was in the Navy, happened to come home to North Dakota on leave. When it came time for him to return to San Diego, he asked me if I would like to ride along on the trip back. That meant I would have to fly back to North Dakota. It was a great trip and also was my first trip to California, we went out to San Francisco and down the coast to an apartment in Del Mar where Curtis was living at the time.

My flight home from San Diego to Bismarck, North Dakota required stops in Denver and Rapid City, South Dakota. Upon arriving in Denver, the first stop, I scrambled to find my way to the next gate where the flight to Rapid City was to board. When I found the gate waiting area, there were only a few people waiting, but there was a guy attracting a lot of attention. A bunch of young folks were getting autographed pictures from him. I picked a seat in the same row in the waiting area, and when most of the autograph seekers had left, the guy asked me if I wanted an autographed picture. I said "sure." I had never heard of Doug "the ragin' Cajun" Kershaw until returning to North Dakota and asking some folks about him.

When the flight was ready to board, Doug was fumbling with a briefcase and multiple fiddle cases and he asked me if I would help him carry some things. I said "sure." Back then, the gate that we were boarding from, required us to go outside and up the stairs of the plane and there were separate boarding stairs for coach and for first class. Doug was leading me up the stairs for first class and I tried to tell him I didn't have a first class ticket. He said not to worry. The attendant checking tickets at the door looked at my ticket, and was shaking her head, but Doug said "Oh, its OK, he's with me." Doug was headed to Rapid City for a concert, so I rode next to him in first class from Denver to Rapid City.

We had great conversation and of course he was unlike anything this old Dakota farm boy had ever known. I got to hear much of his story so I was anxious to learn more. At that time, I wasn't much into Nashville artists. Our band, *Young Imagination,* had just recently released our record and I couldn't resist telling him about it. Of course, he had no idea that it was a "rock" record and a lot different than his music, but he took a lot of interest in what I was doing and was genuinely concerned about my future. He said "you know, if you are really serious and passionate about your career in the music business, you should get off this plane with me and go with me to Nashville." I was stunned and confused, and for a moment tempted, but my Mom and Dad and my girlfriend had driven 180 miles and were waiting at the Bismarck airport for me to arrive. I could not see myself, a 19-year old kid, getting off that plane and blowing off college which was to begin in about a week.

But now, I always wonder…..What if….

Chapter Eight

A Special Meeting With Kris Kristofferson

Kris Kristofferson was having some great success in the early seventies, hit songs, movies, and touring. He was a well-respected singer-songwriter who had captured my attention. On a cold January night in 1974, in Bismarck, North Dakota, his and my paths crossed. I was still a young impressionable college music student at Dickinson State University, and a singer-songwriter excited about getting out on my own in the music business. About a month before, I had completed a recording session in Bismarck, which was produced by the now famous Christian producer, Greg Nelson.

My uncle, Clarence Walth, who thought my recordings were pretty good, happened to know the general manager of the Bismarck Civic Center where a number of national touring acts would come to perform. Kris Kristofferson was doing a concert there, and I was invited as a guest to the concert, AND an opportunity to meet Kris. Of course, I was anxious to meet Kris and play some of my new recordings for him. Back in those days, I had no cassette player, and the only way Kris would be able to hear my songs, was for me to bring my reel-to-reel tape deck with a set of headphones. So, I lugged that tape deck with me to the concert and placed it on the floor under my seat. At the completion of the concert, the general manager took me to Kris's dressing room where I would meet Kris and Billy Swan, who was touring with Kris.

Before entering the dressing room, I waited for Kris to sign a hand full of autographs for the few folks who found the way to his dressing room. They were being watched by a security guard. In the meantime, the general manager who had escorted me to the area, left to take care of other business. When Kris was done signing the autographs, I followed him into the room, and realized I was being followed by the security guard. Thinking I was about to be removed from the room, I was mentally preparing my defense, but the security guard walked right past me and pulled out a pad and pencil and also asked Kris for an autograph. After granting that request, Kris dismissed the security guard, Billy Swan left the room, and Kris and I were alone to talk.

I plugged in my reel-to-reel recorder to play my tape for Kris, which he so graciously agreed to listen to. I can still remember Kris leaning forward over the table, and holding both hands over the earpieces on the headphones, with his eyes closed, as he was listening. After listening, Kris said he thought I wrote great melodies, and he encouraged me to get more personally connected to my lyrics. His advice, to this day, still pushes me to dig deeper within myself when I'm working on my songwriting ideas.

Then, I asked him about his career, and he began telling me his life story, most of which I had not known at that time. He talked about his previous career, education, military, family, divorce, being a Rhodes Scholar, the helicopter incident at Johnny Cash's house, etc. I hung on every word as he described his passion about the music and the songwriting, the decisions that brought him to Nashville, and the odd jobs he did to stay alive. As he talked about the frustrations and the heartbreak, I started to sense a sad and troubled story and I began to wonder where this story would lead. I was thinking maybe he would express some regret for all of the sacrifices he endured from his passionate pursuit of his singer-songwriter career, and try to dissuade me from my interest in the music business. But after completing what seemed to be an especially tragic and heartbreaking part of the story, he paused…..his eyes had sort of a moist, glazed contentment as he turned to me and said…… "after all of the hard times I've had in this business…..It was ALL WORTH IT!!!" That look in his eyes, I will never forget, and Kris's words will stay with me for the rest of my life.

My transition to Nashville a few years ago was not an easy one, my wife and son and I walked away from everything in Colorado to pursue my life and my calling as a singer-songwriter. When there are times when I don't think I can go on, I remember Kris and his words, "It was all worth it" and I put one foot in front of the other and forge onward.

I still have a long road ahead of me, but I believe……I believe because of people like Kris who have made a difference in my life. I tell this story in hopes it might make a difference in someone else's life who struggles with their calling, what ever that calling may be. I think I owe it to Kris to pass it on.

In January, 2009, 35 years after meeting Kris and his friend Billy Swan, I ran into Billy at The Listening Room Café, in Nashville, during a songwriter night hosted by my friend, Garth Shaw. Billy wasn't sure if he remembered meeting me, but he remembered being there with Kris that night in 1974.

Since that encounter with Kris in January, 1974, I have not seen Kris again, but I hope to be able to thank him in person one day.

Chapter Nine

Ronnie Milsap And The Power of Music

The power of music, what an awesome thing! It was Denver, Colorado, 1979 – the first time Sandy and I lived there. I had recently become a Ronnie Milsap fan and Ronnie was scheduled to appear at a Denver area show club called "The Turn Of The Century" where a number of well-known acts were performing in those days.

Ronnie, a country singer, had a little pop and rock side to him and was sometimes crossing over to "top 40" radio where I was exposed to his music. As a melodic singer-songwriter myself, I loved the melodies and big choruses usually found in the songs that he recorded. When I got word of his Denver show I hurried out to buy tickets for Sandy and myself.

The show was on a Saturday night and that morning I awoke with a bad case of stomach flu. Confident that my sickness would be short-lived, I wasn't too worried about the possibility of missing the Ronnie Milsap show that night. But, as the day wore on, I was getting sicker and constantly spending time in the bathroom relieving my stomach of its contents (yes, I was puking my guts out). As the time grew near for the concert I became concerned, even though Sandy assured me it wouldn't be the end of the world if we stayed home, I was determined not to miss the show.

The time arrived for us to depart for the club so I went to the bathroom and threw up one last time (hopefully) and we set out for the show. The trip wasn't too bad, but as we arrived at the club, I was feeling the urge to be sick again. We were seated at our table and were advised that the show included a two-drink minimum. Now, the last thing I wanted at that moment was a drink! However, I ordered a plain Coke and began gently sipping on the glass. I swear, if time could ever have moved more slowly, I couldn't have imagined it. I told myself, if I can just hang on to hear one song, maybe this agony would be worthwhile. It was then I realized there was an opening act, a comedian. Somehow jokes are not that funny when all you can think about is not spraying people at your table with recycled Coke. I made it through the comedian, and through the intermission.

The situation was becoming critical, I felt that at any moment I may need to spring for the door. I kept reminding myself, just make it through one song. Ronnie finally took the stage.

Ronnie had a full ensemble of musicians and, additionally, had three background singers. My anticipation for the performance grew and I was starting to think less about being sick. Ronnie's opening song was "Almost Like A Song" and it started slowly and sweetly, it was washing over me, I thought if this was the only song I would hear, it was definitely worth hearing. Then, it happened. When Ronnie came to the chorus and before he sang "now my broken heart," those background vocalists hit a three-part chord on "ahhh." The sound absolutely took me to a musical place I had never experienced. If there is music in heaven, it must be just like what I heard in that magical transforming moment.

Sick? Not after that moment! We stayed and enjoyed the entire concert……and both encores. I was able to drink both Cokes. My lousy day turned into one of most enjoyable and memorable evenings of my life.

After the conclusion of the show as we walked to our car I said "Aw, what the heck, lets go out for pizza and beer." The music had cured me.

Chapter Ten

Bowling
And The Music Business

When I was a kid, both of my parents belonged to bowling leagues so it was perfectly natural that I would develop an interest in bowling. This was back in the day that the small bowling alleys where my Dad bowled still had manual pinsetters where kids were employed to set the pins in the pinsetters between each rolling of the ball.

The first recollection of my bowling career was when I was about eight years old and I would walk up to the line and roll the ball with both hands. Before long I was able to bowl like the grownups and actually knock down a few pins. The bowling center in Scranton started a youth league when I was twelve or thirteen years old and at this point, I was getting to be a pretty formidable bowler for my age and size.

When I was in high school, I was invited to be a member of my Dad's bowling team and finally in my senior year, I had a higher bowling average than my Dad. I may have had the highest average on the team, but I couldn't be certain after all these years.

My early college years were hectic and filled with music and other activities, so bowling sort of took a back seat for a couple years. One of my relatives invited me to bowl on a team in Dickinson during my junior year so I decided to return to the sport. Bowling was a pretty regular thing during the

Dickinson years (1974-1983) but moving to Denver in 1983 imposed about a five year hiatus and we didn't resume until about 1988.

By the time I was out of high school in 1970, my bowling average per game was about 165. Throughout the Dickinson years, my average was also about 165. After resuming bowling in Denver, in 1990 my average was STILL about 165. The more the average stayed the same, the more frustrated I became. I always believed I had the physical ability to be a better bowler, but I never seemed to improve.

In 1990, a guy named Bruce Johnston started bowling in our league at Celebrity Fun Center in Denver. He was very good, we struck up a friendship, and he somehow inspired me to start on a quest to be a better bowler. Celebrity Fun Center was closing down, so together we moved over to Heather Ridge Lanes and Sandy & I and Bruce were on the same team. From Bruce, I learned about the differences in the materials and surfaces of bowling balls. I learned about bowling lane conditions, and all of the other factors that were required to average more than 165. I didn't yet realize it, but the biggest factor is really mental conditioning.

Little by little, I began to improve. I upgraded my bowling ball....every year. I carefully analyzed how the oil was spread on the lanes, and how it changed from night to night, and even from game to game. Adjustments were always required, and above all else, a positive mental attitude was required. I studied the bowlers who were consistently out performing me. I soon realized that the better I bowled, a camaraderie developed between myself and the best bowlers in the league. We became friendly rivals, and when we bowled against one another we were constantly sizing each other up and poking fun at each other.

I think it was the rivalry and the acceptance of my fellow passionate bowling peers that began to build my confidence. I learned to resist the intimidation factor and to maintain focus. In one season, I jumped from a 165 average to a 185 average! Little by little over the next few seasons my average per game climbed to over 200.

Bowling is a game of skill, but it is a very mental exercise. In addition to knowing the game and analyzing equipment, lane conditions, and other bowlers, one must be continually focused on the task at hand. You line yourself up, and when you begin the approach to the foul line, you have to be totally consumed in the moment and focused on where to lay the ball down and the degree of spin to release it with. The follow through, and envisioning the line that the ball needs to follow to the pins, is critical. Any distraction or negative thought at that moment will impact the outcome of the result.

Now, in addition, there is the intimidation factor among you and the other top bowlers, especially if you are bowling against their team. Sometimes this is subtle and subconscious, but it is definitely a factor in the outcome of each other's score. Kind of hard to explain, but you have to learn to use it and deal with it. Other top bowlers are consciously or subconsciously working on intimidating you, and you have to resist and use your confidence and your own personal intimidation tactics (within reason) to gain power over them.

In the spring of 2000, I finished the year with a 207 bowling average, which was the highest for the league. I was proud, and the confidence that it inspired in me went way beyond bowling. It was a lesson in life.

How is bowling related to the music business? I realized that if I could use my passion for bowling to go from a 165 average to a 207 average, I should be able to use the passion for my music to accomplish even greater things. I also realized the reverse, taking actions without passion won't get you very far.

I learned the valuable lesson that if you are driven by passion, you can accomplish things that you never realized could be possible. I learned that you can look back and be proud of your accomplishments, but always strive to do bigger and better things. What about the intimidation factor? Yes, it applies in the music business as well, and probably any other competitive business. In the process of performing, it is a little more subtle, more a process of maintaining your confidence and composure (don't let them ever see you sweat). There are many confident appearing performers, but everyone gets a little unnerved from time to time.

I now realize there are always going to be people better than me and people who are not as good, but the confidence can make you stand out in the crowd. Being prepared, maintaining focus, and performing every moment, every note, and every word to the best of your ability…with passion… is all you can do. The rest will take care of itself.

Chapter Eleven

Larry Hogoboom
Not Your Ordinary Friend

Many people come in and out of our lives. In our younger days, sometimes we don't give too much thought to the people we meet and the friends we keep and the ones who sometimes tend to fade into history. Are there any real coincidences in life? Or do things usually happen for a reason? We will never know the answers for sure, but somehow, our meeting Larry Hogoboom still seems like more than a coincidence to me. Sometimes things happen in ways that you could never conceive of, and one has to be in awe of these circumstances and be thankful for them.

My wife Sandy and I were married in December of 1976 and moved to Denver Colorado with some friends shortly after Christmas that year. We found a small apartment on the third floor of an apartment complex off Harlan Street in the small Denver community of Edgewater. We were moving into apartment number 307, and in all of the madness of the moving process, we hardly noticed the pile of newspapers setting in front of the door at apartment number 308 next door. After settling in and a few days had passed, we were now aware of the growing pile of newspapers, and wondered what was happening in the next door apartment. All we knew was that the sign on the door said "Hogoboom," and since my mother's cousin in Bowman, North Dakota was married to a

"Hogoboom," I was curious about the name. We were relieved when our neighbor, who was apparently away on a trip, finally returned and we had the opportunity to meet him.

Our new neighbor, Larry Hogoboom, was an outgoing friendly sort of guy. He told us he was in sales, so his personality sort of fit that profile. Since he was right next door, we saw a lot of him the first couple months while Sandy and I were looking for jobs and so he started to be a pretty good friend. I asked him if he was related to any "Hogobooms" in North Dakota, he sort of chuckled and said "no." After a few months, to my surprise, he happened to casually mention that his great grandmother had passed away in Bowman, North Dakota. I tried to remind him that I had asked if he was related to anyone there, and he acted like he didn't remember me asking the question. Years later we discovered a possible reason why he was trying to keep a low profile about the North Dakota connection, we'll talk about that later.

As time went on, we got quite close to Larry. He always seemed to have a girlfriend, and we would get together often to socialize. In addition, our good friends Don and Kayleen, who moved with us to Denver, wound up moving back to North Dakota. Larry was the person who seemed to fill the void left by them.

After a year or so, Larry took this new position as a sales manager for the local franchise of the RainSoft Water Treatment Company. He was always bragging about the products and how easy they were to sell and to make money from selling them. I was in a job that seemed to be going nowhere and I began thinking maybe I could be a salesman. Now, I don't know how valid that was, but there really needs to be a salesperson in all of us. Larry was willing to train me and get me going with RainSoft so I was willing to give it a shot. The owner of RainSoft was a very good speaker and motivator, and I was very privileged to be in on the training meetings and to learn and be motivated by him. This experience and the tools I learned there hang with me today in the way I approach my singer-songwriter career as well as other challenges in life. It was a positive mental attitude approach. After a few sales presentations on my own, I learned to intertwine my own personality into the sales script and to observe how people would react to my approach.

After a few months, Larry had the opportunity to start a RainSoft franchise of his own in Billings, Montana. He needed an additional investment to start the franchise and he asked me if I was interested in going in on it with him. In my naïve way of thinking, it seemed like a way to make a lot of money quickly so that I could settle down into my singer-songwriter career and so I eventually agreed. My good friend, Marvin Brown, my *Young Imagination* buddy, lived in Billings, so it seemed to make sense. We were able to borrow money on a second mortgage on our townhouse to make it work.

As one might imagine, partnerships with friends can be a challenge. In fact, it can turn downright disastrous, as it did in our case. With money issues and various other problems, friends can turn to enemies in a heartbeat. After about six weeks, I packed my bags, and as a result, Sandy and I wound up moving back to North Dakota where we settled in Dickinson. When I left Billings, my future relationship with Larry, was very much in doubt.

We were in Dickinson for four years, and other than trying to check on the money I had invested with my old friend Larry, I never communicated with him. His business in Billings eventually failed and Larry moved back to Denver.

As luck would have it, in 1983, the company in Dickinson that I worked for decided to relocate to……Denver! After we were settled back in Denver, I decided to mend fences and track down my old friend Larry.

When I eventually got a hold of him, he was a little reluctant to warm back up to me, but somehow I think both of us had a need to reconnect. During the years we didn't talk, I began to develop a sense of a special connection to him that to this day I don't fully understand. I always remembered the Bowman, North Dakota connection, but wasn't sure what that meant. Even though my Mother's cousin was married to a relative of his, it wasn't like we were blood relatives.

We maintained our relationship with Larry and got together on a pretty regular basis, but sometimes weeks could go by without talking. Summer 1989 was one of these times, we were busy and I was spending some time in North Dakota promoting my album. The North Dakota Centennial Commission chose my song "Dakota, I've Not Forgotten" as an official project for the centennial celebration in 1989, so I was making numerous concert and media appearances that summer.

Also during that summer, Bowman County North Dakota released a new version of the history of families in the county in a book called "Prairie Tales II" and fortunately, my parents bought a copy for us. Late one afternoon, I stumbled on a chapter in the book called "The Hogoboom Family" and began reading. To my surprise, Larry was in the book. As I read along, the first thing I discovered was, that unlike his brother and only sibling, Larry was adopted! For some reason I was stunned by this information, but it got more interesting. A little further along in the chapter, I read that Larry was once married, divorced and had children! I'm thinking, how is it that we have known Larry at this point for almost 13 years and didn't know he was adopted or married or had kids?

At this very moment the phone rang…..It was Larry! I said, "Larry, you are not going to believe this, but I was just reading about you and your family in the Bowman family history book." Larry sort of hesitated in his response and said "so what." I said "the book tells me you are adopted…..and you were married…..AND you have kids!" There was a long silence at the other end of the phone. Finally Larry said "you are mistaken, they must be talking about my brother, Steve." I responded "no Larry, it is real clear, the book also talks about Steve and his family so I know it is you." Well, after much hemming and hawing around, Larry finally confessed that it was true.

Larry didn't want to offer too much information, but little by little we learned that he had moved to Denver shortly before we did in 1976 from Minneapolis after leaving his family. Apparently, he was in hiding due to family related concerns. It all seemed a little strange, but I didn't want to be too judgmental.

As a result of our discovery, an amazing thing happened. Larry contacted his ex-wife back in Minnesota. He then discovered that he had grand children. He made a couple of trips back to Minnesota to visit them and then, his ex-wife actually came to Denver to see him. And we met her! This was actually a very pleasant and memorable experience for all of us, but as time went on, Larry's reconnection with his family faded. I'm not sure exactly why, but it may not have turned out like he expected and he may not have been as well received by his abandoned family as he had hoped. In any case, I felt like this was bordering on a miraculous event that was somehow meant to be and I was happy to have played a part in it. Larry has remained a dear friend to us ever since.

We moved to Nashville, Tennessee in 2002, and in April, 2009, after not seeing him in about 6 years, Larry made a trip to visit us. His father in Virginia had recently passed away. We do talk on the phone from time to time, but seeing him again was like we had never been apart. Larry plans to visit us again.

Larry has certainly been a different sort of friend, we have had our good times and bad. Our personalities are entirely different, Larry is a free and easy kind of guy, and sometimes pretty wild and crazy. In order to keep this story short, we won't go into all of the wild and crazy stuff. That might be a book in itself! Yet, there is something about my relationship with Larry that I still don't understand, why is it that I have been close to him all of these years? Could it be that since he was adopted in North Dakota, maybe he is related more closely than I know? Maybe there is more of this story to be played out in the future.

However, I do believe that it wasn't a coincidence that we met Larry. There must have been a reason, some divine intervention, we must have needed each other in some way. I won't question fate in bringing us together, but am looking forward to what the future may bring because of it.

Chapter Twelve

My Dear Friend And First Producer, Mike Crowley

Due to business pursuits in the mid-1980's, my music career got put on the back burner for awhile. But, it had been too long, I was getting very antsy. I always had the inspiration to record a solo project of my own songs and one of those songs was *"Dakota, I've Not Forgotten."* North Dakota was in the planning stages of their upcoming Centennial Celebration in 1989, and it occurred to me maybe that could be a reason or motivation for me to work on an album.

But I reasoned that to do an album, I needed a producer. Not any old producer, but one who was not only exceptional, but well connected to the industry. In 1988, I went to a special music event at the University of Colorado at Denver (UCD)…where I would eventually become part-time faculty (but that's another story). This event featured Brent Maher, producer of the Judds and others, and the event was attended by many local music people. I approached well-known sound engineer Bill Porter, who was a professor at UCD at the time and asked him if he had any recommendations for producers. Bill said he didn't but he pointed out another person in the room who he said "knew everybody in town". This guy turned out to be Mike Becker so I introduced myself. Mike and I are still close friends.

After briefly describing my music to Mike Becker, he said "you should talk to Mike Crowley, he may be good for your style of music AND he is good friends with John Denver". I thought "JOHN DENVER," that works for me! It took a few weeks, but I finally was introduced to Mike Crowley.

Mike Crowley was a likeable distinguished guy and I really felt comfortable around him. He had a wealth of knowledge and experience in the music business, and I learned that he had been one of the members of "The New Christy Minstrels" in the early 1960's. He went from there to a group called "The Back Porch Majority" and they had a hit song called "Second Hand Man." It was during this period that John Denver was Mike's roommate. In addition to John Denver, Mike also knew and was respected by most of the singers, songwriters, and performers working in California in those days.

The first song Mike and I worked on was "Dakota, I've Not Forgotten." I had written the song in 1979 when Sandy and I first lived in Denver. I had gotten discouraged by the city life and was missing North Dakota, and we then moved back to Dickinson, North Dakota where we lived from 1979 to 1983. It was in 1987, when we were living back in Denver, that I remembered the big centennial celebration that was being planned in North Dakota for the commemoration of 100 years of statehood that began in 1889. I recalled the song and added a line to the bridge and took it to Mike with the idea that maybe I could tie the song in with the upcoming centennial. At that time in my life, the recording that Mike and I did sounded incredible to me. Others thought so also, and in fact, the North Dakota Centennial Commission chose to sanction the song for inclusion in the 1989 Celebration. The Centennial Commission backing led to an incredible run of radio & TV interviews, airplay, and concert appearances. Even considering that my prior music business experience had given me good instincts about marketing and media, I was unprepared for the timing of events that occurred.

After recording "Dakota, I've Not Forgotten," Mike totally fell in love with my song "In Your Eyes." I think he felt it represented the depth of lyric writing that I was capable of producing. It is a song about life's journey and fate's timing in the relationships in our lives. Mike said "you know my old friend John Denver doesn't seem to have a lot new going on these days, maybe he could be interested in recording this song". After sending a copy to John, Mike called him for his impression and John said "I think Randi is a very gifted poetic songwriter", "but the song is not something I could hear myself recording." In those days, I had expectations, I was sure John would say he would love to record my song, especially with Mike's recommendation and support. I was terribly disappointed. I didn't write "poems", I was a "songwriter." It wasn't until many years later that I realized John Denver had given me maybe the biggest compliment he could have given anyone, and looking back today, I take pride in the multiple meanings and depth of thought that goes into the lyrical lines that I write. With the best of my God given talent, I carefully select every word and every line. I will always seek to find a better way or a better delivery, but I celebrate with confidence, the gift of individuality and uniqueness that I was given as a singer-songwriter.

After having *Dakota* and *In Your Eyes* "in the can" I was chomping at the bit to finish my album. The spring and summer was approaching, and with tour dates being set up, I needed to have my album ready to go. Still riding a high from the excitement of the first two recordings, I went to see Mike to schedule another recording session. Earlier, I had given Mike a cassette tape of about 20 songs to consider. But when we got together that day, Mike's first question to me was "what else have you got to record," to which I responded "what about the 20 song tape I gave you?" Mike's comment was "I don't like any of 'em." For me, it was emotionally like going from the top of the highest mountain to being lower than whale dung. Mike said "you need to go write another song like *In Your Eyes*." I went home with my tail between my legs and started writing and re-writing. As a result, most of the rest of that album was newly written. I will be forever thankful for the kick in the pants that Mike gave me.

One little bit of trivia that Mike Crowley told me was a story about how John Denver got his name. Mike's real name was Michael Crumm and John's given name was John Deutschendorf. When Mike and John were working together in California for the New Christy Minstrel organization, their manager, Randy Sparks, informed them that they would have to change their names because "Crumm" and "Deutschendorf" wouldn't work. Mike and John had both recently purchased Samsonite luggage with their initials engraved on the luggage. Mike suggested they use names with the same initials so that they wouldn't have to change the luggage. They came up with "Crowley" and "Denver." That story was recently confirmed in the 2004 book by G. Brown called *Colorado Rocks!: A Half Century of Music in Colorado*.

Unfortunately, Mike Crowley passed away in April 2001 from lung cancer. I know Mike came into my life for a reason and his memory will always be with me. I will strive to pass on the legacy he left for me.

Chapter Thirteen

Oh, Brother...Learning Life While Spinning Out Of Control

In the spring of 1995, I was working part-time for a software company in Denver. It was a sunny, warm and beautiful day and my friend Larry had called to invite me to join him for lunch. My work had been challenging that morning, and I was excited to be leaving for the day and joining Larry for lunch. I left the office and cranked up the radio as I entered the on-ramp to I-25. Alison Krauss was singing "When You Say Nothing At All," one of my favorite songs, as I accelerated onto to the freeway having no idea what was about to happen.

I was leaving the freeway at the next exit, and at the point where the freeway expanded to four lanes, I moved to the right lane and sped up to get around a delivery truck that was lumbering along ahead of me. At this exact moment, the delivery truck decided to move over into the lane I was in. Things were happening so fast I didn't have time to think. I slammed on the brakes and skidded to the right shoulder where I took out a mile marker sign, but was relieved when the truck had also slammed on his brakes and I was able to pull back on the road in front of him.

Just when I thought things were back under control, the car started fishtailing wildly and I was headed into a 180-degree spin. I would later realize that slamming on the brakes with a manual transmission without pushing in the clutch would kill the engine and lock the front wheels. I-25 is always a busy freeway at all hours of the day and not a good place to be losing control of my car! My life was reduced to an "in the moment, slow motion ordeal" where I watched the four lanes of traffic miraculously open up and allow me to skid around and sideways all the way to the median in the middle. I was now stopped and facing the wrong direction looking at four lanes of stopped traffic. After discovering the car was not running, I was able to restart it and pull off again to the far right lane and take my exit. I then discovered that the truck driver had stopped on the ramp, and he apologized for running me off the road and gave me his card.

I spent a few moments alone in the car trying to catch my breath and come to grips with what had just happened to me. This was a spiritual moment. I realized that when my car was spinning around on that freeway, my life was no longer in my hands. Whatever was going to happen to me in that instant was up to God! And you know, as frightful as it was to not be in control of the car, there was a certain calmness that came over me. It was mind boggling to think that all of the movements of those cars had to be just right to prevent me from being in a major accident. It occurred to me that feeling like we are in control of the actions in our lives may really just be an illusion.

I would soon learn that at that very moment while I was spinning on the freeway, my brother Scott was laying in a coma from liver failure at my parents' house in Scranton, North Dakota. Even though he would later regain consciousness, he was fighting a losing battle with Hepatitis C.

Scott was my youngest brother and the third of four siblings. I am the oldest. Scott had his share of struggles with drugs and alcohol, he was an alcoholic. He had been through treatment a couple times without success, but it seemed as though he had finally turned it around enough to be eligible for a liver transplant.

A few weeks after my accident, I spent some time on my Dad's farm where Scott was helping put in the crop. He had recovered well from the coma and was looking good. I wondered if maybe the coma somehow had something to do with his apparent recovering health. He was due to be on a liver transplant list soon, and I was hopeful that he could have a bright future.

Scott was a talented kid. He was always good at sports and was a great drummer. He was in a rock band with me when he was only in the 7th grade and later played drums for us in "The Perkins Family Band." Scott had a great personality and was liked by a lot of people. He was a good communicator, very fond of history, and loved to engage in friendly debates. At one time, his goal was to be a lawyer, and he would have been a good one. Despite his troubles, I had utmost respect for Scott and believed that he just might turn out to be the most successful of us all.

But it was not to be. During the week of July 4, 1995, my brother Scott died from liver failure alone at his apartment in Fargo. He had recently gone back to Fargo to finish his Bachelor's degree at NDSU since he only had one semester left. As fate would have it, all of his close friends and relatives were out of town and no one was available to check on him. His death wasn't discovered for about a week.

I sometimes still find it hard to believe that Scott is gone and I still grieve for him. But, in a way, his death inspired me. I thought about all of his talents that he never got to pursue and realized how short life really is. We have to strive to make the most of every moment, because we never know what tomorrow may bring, or how many tomorrows there will be.

At Scott's funeral, one of his close friends told me that Scott had come to terms with not having long to live and that he didn't want to be a burden on his family. He may have known death was near when he went to Fargo. I think he realized, like I did during my I-25 accident, that his life was in God's hands. All he could do was get on with living out whatever time he had left and make the most of it.

Now, when I think about Scott, I think about the pursuit of my destiny and living every moment like it was my last. Another accident like the one I had on I-25 may not result in the same outcome. I have to go on with my life because Scott would have wanted it that way.

Chapter Fourteen

About the Song: *"When I Think I'm Gonna Fall In Love"*

I write songs about situations in my life or people close to me where I'm caught up in an emotion. After the death of my brother a few years ago, I was left dealing with feelings of loss and abandonment and was touched by observing other family members and friends affected by his death. I'm always searching for the positive side of negative events.

I incorporated the emotion from that setting into the idea for the song *"When I Think I'm Gonna Fall In Love"*. I envisioned how the spouse of a loved one might deal with their loss. On the lighter side, faithful CBS *"Guiding Light"* fans will know of the long-standing relationship between Josh & Reva. Reva has died and come back to life multiple times in the past and each time Josh has struggled through new relationships hanging on to the memories of Reva. Now, as a guy, I hesitate to admit that I watch soap operas, much less get emotionally involved in one, but truth is, sometimes they are a good source of song ideas.

As this song was evolving, I had played a demo of the song for a song critique panel and was told by a well-known and highly regarded professional songwriter that no one would ever "get" this idea and I should rewrite it as a "leaving" song as opposed to having the person's loved one die. He felt that more people could relate to the song if the girl just left the guy and hadn't died. The song would then be more "commercially viable." After careful consideration, I left the song as I originally had written it.

Some time later, I was performing the song at a songwriter show at a local bar. After my set, while I was putting my guitar in its case, I was approached by a guy who had been seated at the bar listening to my songs. He had a few beers, but the emotion of the moment was in the welled-up eyes and the story on his face. He thanked me for doing the song and that it "spoke to him." His wife had recently passed away and he said that "it's hard to understand how that truly feels until it happens to you."

At that moment, I was thanking God for giving me the strength to ignore the advice to change my song to make it more "commercial." It was a reminder to me that my gift of songwriting talent may have a higher purpose. Who knows, that guy may have needed that song at that particular time and I was his Angel of the moment.

Now, I encourage other songwriters to trust their own instincts and I carefully pause to reflect when I'm making comments on other songwriter's songs. The passions and instincts that drive us to write about a heartfelt idea just might come from a higher source.

The song lyrics: *When I Think I'm Gonna Fall In Love*

I always thought that I could fall in love again
It wouldn't be a matter of if, but only when
But, I never knew that it could be so hard
To leave your memory behind
I always thought the pain would go away
In a matter of time

When I think I'm gonna fall in love, you seize my heart again
I'm caught before I fall in love cause your memory's my best friend
It seems before I fall in love, you're the one I compare it to
When I think I'm gonna fall in love, I think of you

I never knew that life could be so tough 'til the Lord took you
Yet, I look for the good in everything, that's my rule
But now, when I really need someone
My heart is in your hands
Your memory always seems to find a way
To change my plans
    (chorus)
Maybe it's just you watchin' down from above
Helping me to find the right one to love
    (chorus)

Chapter Fifteen

The Last Harvest
The Story Behind The Song

My Dad, Robert W (Bud) Perkins, grew up in the 1920's and 1930's on a farm homesteaded by his father in Southwestern North Dakota. Except for spending a year in Los Angeles in 1940-41, he lived and worked his entire life on that farm where he grew up. Surviving the 30's, he had a tremendous work ethic and will to succeed.

As I got out on my own and started pursuing my life and my dreams, I made the assumption that my Dad had many dreams and goals of his own that he never had the chance to pursue. I imagined he saw farming as the only thing he knew or was qualified to do, and after having a family, just resigned himself to remaining there on the farm making a living and supporting his family. He was just trying to do the "right thing."

I was exposed to commercial music at an early age, performing and writing songs. I began my working life and business skills playing in rock bands during the summer breaks from college. It became so much a part of me that I had to follow that dream no matter what. Growing up in North Dakota, the music business was only a distant vision, not seeming real or something to make a living doing. I felt the prevailing wisdom, "the right thing," was to follow a career where I could be more easily employed and make a good living. I became an Certified Public Accountant with a Master of Business Administration degree, moved to the city, and tried many different jobs, hoping to one day make enough money to spend time writing songs and getting into the music business. After 20 years of career and financial disappointments, I realized that I could never attain my musical goals that way, nor would I ever make any money.

In 2000, my Dad retired from farming and had an auction sale for the machinery and equipment that he no longer needed. I attended the auction sale, just to see that farm and equipment I had worked on as a kid one last time. I saw my Dad as a successful and contented farmer, who after setting aside his other dreams and goals, managed to overcome the hardships of farming and be a well-respected man in his home town.

After an emotional day of watching people buy and take that machinery from the farm, I decided to ask my Dad about the dreams and goals of his youth. "If you could start all over and follow your dream, what would it be?" I asked. Without hesitation, my Dad said….. "farming WAS my dream."

Since that sunny autumn day in October 2000, my life has never been the same. It was at that moment I realized that the example my Dad set for me wasn't what I thought. He did "the right thing" by following his dream of farming. Now, I know I have to follow the passion in my heart for the music business as if someone's life depends on me. That someone could be my son. *"The Last Harvest"* is the example we set for our kids by following our dreams.

THE LAST HARVEST
(The Song Lyrics)

A survivor of the thirties, he held on to his ground
He was never rich or famous, but he was well known in his town
He walked the straight and narrow line that led him to this day
Now, the setting prairie sun is shining on his place

It is the last harvest, he's as proud as he can be
At this auction sale he said goodbye to his machinery
Life is hard, but he survived the best way that he could
Now, he's reapin' what he sowed, and life is good

He has a wife and four kids, and I am one of those
From where I stand, his just might be the greatest story ever told
He's been a husband and a father, yet he lived his life his way
Farming was his dream and he learned to make it pay

It is the last harvest, he's as proud as he can be
At this auction sale he said goodbye to his machinery
Life is hard, but he survived the best way that he could
Now, he's reapin' what he sowed, and life is good

I have chosen a different road, it's the city life I lead
But, the heart and soul of this farmer's dream is alive inside of me

It is the last harvest, ***I'M*** *as proud as I can be*
At this auction sale ***I*** *said goodbye to his machinery*
Life is hard, but ***I'LL*** *survive the way he knew I would*
Now, ***I'M*** *reapin' what he sowed, and life is good*

- - -

Song Notes:

    I want to offer a discussion here of the very special messages contained in this song. *"The Last Harvest"* has at least three different meanings in the song, the obvious is that it is literally the last harvest because my Dad was retiring. It was also a "harvest" of converting the machinery, a material thing, to cash for a better use. Finally, what it all really comes down to, is that my Dad followed his dream and calling, and set an example for my siblings and I, and for the future generations of our families. That legacy is truly *"The Last Harvest."*

    When I am 78 years old, and my son asks "Dad, if you could start your career over, what would your dream really have been?" I would say……

Chapter Sixteen

2nd Graders Dig Singer-Songwriters Too!

When I was in the 2nd grade in a small country school in North Dakota, I didn't know what a singer-songwriter was, much less have a chance to hear one in person. I don't even remember whether I paid much attention to songs on the radio. We did sing in school, so I was familiar with some children's songs of the day.

While my son Clark was in the 2nd grade in Denver, his teacher learned that I was a singer-songwriter who was making frequent trips to Nashville and asked me if I would like to come by and play for the class. Of course, I agreed, but I had some reservations about playing for an audience that young. I was pretty sure that they wouldn't be too interested and probably wouldn't be paying attention. I certainly had enough experiences playing in noisy clubs where people weren't paying attention, so I was sure that I could handle it in any case.

I don't really do children's songs, but I have written a number of songs about my younger days, and about my son, so I planned a little program around those songs. I prepared interesting introductions of the songs, so that if they were listening, the lyrics might make some sense.

Most of the kids knew I was Clark's dad, so not much introduction was required from the teacher. I was quite impressed how they gathered around in semi-circles in front of me and were in innocent anticipation of what this little program was going to entail.

As I spoke, giving them some background about myself and what I was doing, I was amazed at how well behaved they were and how attentive they became. They seemed to be in awe as I would introduce the songs. When I sang, they would appear to hang on every word. My program lasted for half a dozen songs, and not once did I lose their attention. I finally wrapped up the program and thanked them all for listening. They immediately got to their feet and want to come and meet me and comment to me in their own way about their listening experience.

As it turns out, it was an incredible experience for me! I was absolutely overwhelmed by this 2nd grade audience. I think too many times, we underestimate children. After all, they are real people too. They are our future generation. I came to realize that the ones of us who help shape their lives at these tender ages really can make a difference in our nation's future.

The following year, I came back to play for them when they were 3rd graders and had a much similar experience. Not only were they a great audience, but some of them remembered the words to my songs! Now, that really got me thinking! How important it is that these kids get exposed to meaningful music and arts at this early age. I would like to think that I shared a meaningful experience with them. Who knows, I may have become an important part of the soundtrack of their lives!

Thank God for kids!

Chapter Seventeen

Jock Bartley From FireFall
A Regular Guy

I was a regional coordinator for the Nashville Songwriters Association International (NSAI) from 1999 to 2002 while I was living in Denver, Colorado. To my surprise one day, Jock Bartley, a founding member of the 70's band FireFall, called me after finding my number on the NSAI website. Jock lives in the Denver area, but I never had met him. He was looking to possibly do a seminar or some teaching for the NSAI chapter.

FireFall was a favorite band of mine in the mid-70's and became one of my influences. I could hardly imagine that twenty some years later I would be getting a phone call from Jock Bartley! We had lunch a few times and became friends and I discovered we had a lot in common.

I hosted a local songwriter show in Denver called Songwriters LIVE! for most of 2001 and had urged Jock to perform with me. He always respectfully declined or had a scheduling conflict. However, in September 2001, Jock was hosting a songwriter event at the Taste Of Colorado, which is a huge event held in downtown Denver every year. Jock invited me to be a part of the show. Now, I had played some big shows before with bands, but usually I'm performing solo in intimate settings in clubs or coffee houses. When I looked out from the stage at what appeared to be a sea of people, I had visions of Woodstock in my head. As a solo singer-songwriter, this was by far the biggest audience I could have imagined at that time. As we were tuning up and getting prepared to start the show, Jock, who was sitting next to me, leaned over to me and whispered "I'm sure this is no big deal to you since you play out solo every week, but I am always performing with a band and this crowd scares the sh*t out of me!".

    I looked at Jock and smiled. A warm sense of confidence came over me. It made me realize that all of us performers have to deal with audiences in our own way and sometimes the butterflies can get the best of us. We are all just people dealing with insecurities like every other human being. Now, when I get nervous about a show, I use that memory of Jock's words to quiet my anxiety.

Chapter Eighteen

You're Just Gonna Have To Deal With Aubrey Collins

On a hot August, 2000 night in Denver, Colorado at a Jana Stanfield concert, Aubrey Collins was plucked from the audience to sing with Jana on stage. It was my first glimpse of the 12-year-old feisty and fearless singer who would capture my passions and lead to my relentless promotional pursuit of creating a Nashville buzz on her behalf. Living in Denver at that time, I had been making numerous visits to Nashville since 1997 and knowing that Aubrey Collins was a special talent, I set aside some of my own interests as a singer-songwriter to dedicate my experience and energy to her. I saw a little of myself in Aubrey, and wanted her to have some of the opportunities I never had when I grew up as a young performer.

Aubrey's vocal coach from age 8 to 12, Stuart Whitmore, introduced me to Aubrey and her mother Susan. Stuart asked if I would pitch songs to her for a CD he was producing, and Aubrey chose to record my song called "Take Me By The Heart" which I co-produced with Stuart. From this introduction, a close relationship developed between myself, Aubrey and her family.

In the summer of 2001, Aubrey's mother Susan had contacted me regarding assisting Aubrey with her desire to write songs. Aubrey had been writing pieces of lyrics and poems, but had never completed a song. I began coaching her on songwriting on a weekly basis to provide her with school credit (she was enrolled at Laurel Springs, a California distance learning school). Knowing that it was essential to have a musical tool to help write melodies and chord progressions, I helped her learn some basics on her guitar. She had a Washburn guitar but had never really learned to play it. Upon getting a foundation on guitar, the songs started coming quickly, and I looked forward to meeting with her every week to hear the new stuff she had written. She progressed very rapidly. Her songs were sort of simple at first, but very insightful for her age. Many songwriting pros probably would have tried to impose certain songwriting "rules" on Aubrey's process, but I was determined to encourage her to find her own creative way as a singer-songwriter.

For most of 2001, I hosted a songwriter show in Denver called *"Songwriters LIVE!"* After Aubrey had written only about three complete songs and became more confident on guitar, I invited her to play in a round with me in the show. This was not exactly an amateur show, Aubrey was positioned between me and Les Fradkin, the guitar player for the 70's band, *Edison Lighthouse* (Love Grows Where My Rosemary Goes,and other 70's hits). Now, as a veteran songwriter and performer, I had heard most everyone make excuses before they sang like "I haven't performed this in a while" or "I just got over a cold". I have been guilty of that a few times also, but as a host of a songwriter show, the many difference excuses were getting annoying. When I heard Aubrey start out with "I just finished this song today……" I thought, great, here we go again, another excuse. But, as she continued, she said "….I may screw up this song, **but you're just gonna have to deal with it!!!!!**" I could hardly believe my ears! The look on Les Fradkin's face was priceless. I looked over at Aubrey with a smile and gave her a thumbs up knowing that a star was in the making. Aubrey completed the song fearlessly and flawlessly…..and I was proud.

Aubrey went on to spend time in Nashville and California working on her songwriting and performing career. As of this writing, she has been on national television with NBC's *"Most Talented Kid"* in 2003 and on ABC's *"The One: The Making Of A Music Star"* in 2006. She spent most of 2007 as the lead singer for the country band *"Trick Pony"* and currently lives in Nashville.

Chapter Nineteen

Randi...Please Stand Up!

This is a tale about unexpected surprises and controlling expectations. I will always be thankful to Rob Crosby for his recognition and respect.

Over the years, I have worked hard on entertainment projects and events because I believed it was the right thing to do, not only for myself, but for others as well. My passion as a singer-songwriter would be the driving force behind these events and I was sure that creating opportunities for others would also be beneficial for me. Prior to moving to Nashville in 2002, I was the Denver coordinator for the Nashville Songwriters Association International (NSAI). My job as coordinator was primarily to hold monthly meetings, but I felt an obligation to generate as much activity for my fellow songwriters in Colorado as possible.

I was always looking for opportunities to bring Nashville songwriters to Denver to perform. For years, I had been a fan of Rob Crosby, who was a successful singer-songwriter in Nashville and had a record deal as an artist in the early 1990's. In 1999, I was fortunate to have the opportunity to meet Rob and get to know him. Rob had mentioned to me that he made a trip to Denver each year to participate in the annual Make-A-Wish Celebrity fund raising event along with a number of other songwriters. I had an idea that it might be possible to get Rob and an additional couple of these songwriters to do a show for our NSAI chapter while they were in town, so I mentioned my plan to Rob. Rob liked the idea and said that the songwriters were always looking for additional exposure as well.

In the spring of 2000, I put my plan into action. I found a venue and set a date following the Make-A-Wish event so that the songwriters would stay an extra day to do the performance. Rob recruited Billy Montana and Jon Vezner to do the show with him. About a week before the show, Rob called and said that Bo Cottrell, the director of the Denver Make-A-Wish organization, had found out about our show and insisted that it be canceled. Rob apologized and said that he felt compelled to cancel the show to appease the director.

Of course, canceling the show was a big blow to me since I had put in so much time and effort to put it together. However, Rob suggested that we plan one for the following year and make it part of the Make-A-Wish event and he gave me Bo Cottrell's phone number. I contacted Bo and we eventually had a meeting. Bo embraced the songwriter show idea after meeting me and learning more about my role in the local music scene.

In 2001, I founded and began hosting a weekly all original songwriter show called "Songwriters LIVE!" at a club named McDonough's. This club was set up well for songwriter shows and I felt it was a great place to hold the upcoming Make-A-Wish songwriter event in June, 2001. Everything came together as planned. Rob Crosby, Billy Montana, and Jon Vezner did the show and it was a tremendous success. We raised money for Make-A-Wish and many of the NSAI members were able to attend. We were also pleased that many of the celebrities in town for the Make-A-Wish weekend stayed to attend our event. A good time was had by all and I was pleased and honored to have coordinated this special songwriter show. I had grand expectations of making this show an annual affair.

In March of 2002, I was again gearing up for a new show. I contacted Rob to discuss the plans and maybe bring additional songwriters to the show. Unfortunately, Rob informed me that Make-A-Wish was planning to take over the show and hold it as part of their regular weekend events. Again, I was bummed. I grumbled to a few people about how unfair it was to put in a lot of time and energy and basically have someone take over your idea. I should have immediately called Bo Cottrell, but I didn't.

About a week before the Make-A-Wish weekend in 2002, Rob called me and said that I needed to contact Bo Cottrell because he had enquired about engaging my help for the songwriter show. So, I called Bo. He was thankful to hear from me and apologized for not calling, he needed help with some details on the songwriter show that they were planning to hold at a country club. In addition, he mentioned that he had a VIP table set up for me and my guests! So, now I'm thinking, thank God I called him, and I was feeling a little stupid for grumbling.

This 2002 Make-A-Wish songwriter show was a much bigger and more formal event than I would have envisioned. Rob, Billy, and Jon all performed again as did Jon's wife, Kathy Mattea. There were a number of VIP tables and most of the celebrities attended the event. It was even hosted by Bob Goen from "Entertainment Tonight." My VIP table was front and center where I was honored to be among such distinguished quests!

Bob Goen made a great MC, but as he explained how the show came about, it sounded like it was all Make-A-Wish's idea to feature the songwriters attending their event. Knowing that it came from my idea, I was grumbling again, but only to myself. And then, to my surprise, when it was Rob's turn to perform, he took it upon himself to explain the history of the songwriter show and how it evolved over a few years. Rob announced that it was my idea and that I was the one who was responsible for starting the show! He introduced me and said "Randi…..Please stand up!" What an unexpected surprise and honor! The packed room applauded, and in addition, many of the attending celebrities came over to my table at the end of the show to introduce themselves and thank me.

I almost did not attend this show! I could have gone on thinking Bo Cottrell cut me out of this deal. This was a reminder that it is important for us to willingly be of service and be happy with knowing we did the right thing without having expectations. My only regret was not having enough warning to invite my parents from North Dakota to the show. I'm sure they would have been excited to be there.

I am thankful to Bo Cottrell for allowing me to participate in these shows in 2001 and 2002, and of course, the biggest thank you of all goes to Rob Crosby!

Chapter Twenty

1200 Miles Without Radio…Searching

Searching…..for radio stations, as I drove from Denver to Nashville and back when I first began making those trips in 1997. FM radio stations would carry maybe 50 miles or so and then I would search the frequencies for another suitable station. I got tired of that. On one of those trips, in the middle of Kansas on I-70, I decided to just shut the radio off. Even though I am a music guy, the music was becoming too much like noise. An interesting transformation was taking place, all I had left was the constant hum of the wind and tires on the road, and the focusing of my eyes on the white lines racing toward me.

I began to hear things, it was my innermost soul speaking. Searching…..now, not for radio stations, but searching for me. I don't know if you would call this meditation, or a hypnotic trance or something, but my subconscious mind was definitely engaged. I thought about family, friends, and my roots…..where I came from and where I might be headed. I was beginning to make the connection between the singer-songwriter in me, and all of my thoughts and experiences that have accumulated over the years. It made me believe that my life had a purpose, a destiny. It made me contemplate the meaning of my life, and how we are all inter-related.

Life is a spiritual journey. These passions that drive us have meaning and purpose in leading us down this spiritual road of life, and as we encounter one another on that road, we have a mutual connection.....a crossroads of destiny. I now think that every time I meet someone, or encounter a situation, I might be somebody's angel.....or they might be mine. They will be better served if I can understand who I am, and how I fit into the universe.

Now, I would never encourage anyone not to listen to music! After all, as a singer-songwriter, it is important to me that there are some listeners out there that can connect with me. But, there is a time for listening to music, and there is a time for quiet...both can sooth our soul. Years ago, I felt that some popular music was becoming noise, becoming less meaningful, and maybe even becoming a negative influence to our younger generation. I wanted to do my part, to make a difference, in presenting music as a more positive influence in the lives of our children.

During my own soul searching on these trips, it occurred to me that maybe that noise and clutter in the lives of our younger generation will prevent them from connecting with their own innermost selves, and divert them from finding their destiny.

Because of the nature of my music, common wisdom says it would appeal to adults who can more identify with the time in which I have lived, but I have always believed that if my music could get introduced to college generation kids, and younger kids as well, the spiritual message it contains would as easily touch them as it would their parents. We have to give our younger generations more credit for the depth of understanding they can achieve.

Searching while on the road to Nashville helped me on the road to centering my life, making me understand that the singer-songwriter soul in me was, for better or for worse, going to be in the center of everything that I do. Not that family or anything else in my life was less important, but that mine and my family's lives could be better understood and lived more fully by facing the reality of who I am.

We can all live fuller lives if we can define what we do by who we are…..rather than defining who we are by what we do.

Chapter Twenty One

The Second Coming Of Mark Nelson

It was Monday, January 15, 2007. The day started out like any other winter's day in Nashville, Tennessee, but sometime in the mid-morning I experienced a reality-shattering event. It was like from the depths of the universe, the hand of God reached out and slapped me to get my attention.

This story actually began back in the spring of 1975, when as a young man about to graduate from undergraduate school in Dickinson, North Dakota, I was having lunch with my parents at the local Woolworth store. Even though I was receiving my degree in business administration, I expressed to my Mom & Dad that I knew that I must pursue my career as a singer-songwriter in the music business. After recently winning the male vocalist award at the regional Country Jamboree in Dickinson, my confidence was at an all-time high, and my first wife and I had decided to move to California where I would attend a recording arts and music industry school for a year. My parents were skeptical and somewhat concerned about me, but I asked for their prayers and understanding. To this day, they have always been supportive and have respected my talents and decisions.

As life goes, things happen. Before we set out for California, my first wife and I split up, and at this time in my life I was feeling a little lost and alone and vulnerable. I just couldn't see myself going to a far away place alone were I didn't know anyone. My Mom, sensing that I was torn about my music, family and what I was about to do, suggested that maybe I find a job locally and work for awhile to maybe get myself back on track. Her advice sort of came as a relief, I thought maybe it would be better to take some time and for the time being, not venture too far into the unknown. In September, 1975, I decided to move to Bismarck, North Dakota to look for a job, and I stayed with my aunt and uncle until I could find a place of my own.

Job-hunting was an interesting challenge. I had a business degree but really didn't know what I wanted to look for. After all, I was really just a singer-songwriter looking for a way to make a living until I could get my music career going. I knew that I had some good business intuition from the success that I had attained promoting and playing with *"Young Imagination,"* the rock band I formed along with my brother and a couple of friends of ours during my early college years. Other than music, my only previous work experience was working on the farm with my Dad.

I ran across a classified ad in the Bismarck Tribune by a local non-profit organization that was looking for a "fiscal officer." I wasn't sure at the time what that job would entail, but I went for an interview. The folks I met there were really friendly and I seemed like a good fit for them. They were interested in hiring me but told me I would first have to interview with Mark H Nelson who was the new Executive Director and was in charge of the new programs that were being funded by the state. Mark took the staff's recommendation and hired me.

Mark H Nelson was, to say the least, an interesting character, very outspoken, smart, and fearless. I guess he was the kind of person you either liked or didn't, but he and I got along great. Mark was a self-taught kind of guy, in fact he hadn't even completed a high school education, but he was very worldly and commanded respect in all that he did. He was also the kind of boss that wanted to get to know the people who worked with him. I felt very comfortable telling him about my musical career and goals, he did not make me feel like my job was at stake for having other dreams. He also respected my musical and creative talents and encouraged me to believe in myself and follow my calling, whatever that turned out to be. Mark wasn't much older than me, and looking back now, I think we were both searching for our true meaning in life.

This "fiscal officer" thing turned out to be an accounting job. I was actually kind of thankful for the experience at something new and it added some order to my life. When I take on a project, I always strive to be the best and this was no exception. Little did I know that I would be attached to accounting for many years to come. After getting comfortable with the job, I entertained the idea of taking the CPA exam and talked to Mark Nelson to get his advice. Mark very sincerely explained that because of my musical aspirations, it might be more fitting to take a general approach and get an MBA degree. He said that an MBA degree was one of his personal goals.

Our organization was developing offices in two other locations, Dickinson (where I went to college) and Jamestown, North Dakota. We were hiring accountants for those offices and I was part of the interviewing process. Sandy, who would become my wife, was the person we hired in the Dickinson office. After a few weeks of working with Sandy, we began dating and after a relatively short time, we became engaged. We set a wedding date for December 17, 1976 and as our adventurous spirits began to take over, we decided to both leave our jobs and move to Denver, Colorado after the wedding. The first chapter with Mark H Nelson had come to an end.

The following years found me in and out of accounting jobs, actually eventually passing the CPA exam and becoming a CPA. If that wasn't enough, I took Mark Nelson's advice and went back to school and got an MBA in 1987. Sandy and I lived in Denver for 2 years, moved back to North Dakota for 4 years, then back to Denver for 19 years. For me, it was a frivolous attempt to find a way to use my business and accounting experience to "make a lot of money" so I could eventually get into the music business full time. My singer-songwriter roots, the depth of which I didn't always understand, went with me everywhere I went, always writing, always performing, and getting involved with musical organizations and events. After the death of my brother Scott in 1995, and a scary event with an accounting client of mine, my gut feeling was telling me that I needed to follow my passions and that I was never going to make enough money at something I wasn't passionate about. I began traveling to Nashville, Tennessee in 1997 on a regular basis to network and to make connections for my songs and my artistic talents. Part of my plan was to get into artist development and management to learn more about the music business in order to create outlets for my songs, thinking I could use my business and accounting expertise to "backdoor my way into the industry".

After about 25 trips to Nashville from Denver, mostly by car, without any measurable success, I came to the realization that I would have to either move to Nashville or stop making trips. Sandy and Clark eventually agreed and we all moved to Nashville in the summer of 2002. The years 2002 to 2007 were an uphill battle as we had basically walked away from everything in Denver to build a new life in Nashville in the music business. Upon arrival in Nashville and realizing I needed to bring in some money to offset what I wasn't making as a songwriter, I began looking for jobs. When I think about working for money, I think about....you guessed it, "accounting jobs." Looking for jobs in the music industry and holding myself out as "an accountant" is an interesting proposition. People tend not to see accountants as creative people and I eventually found myself with an identity crisis. When people introduced me as "an accountant," I'd want to say "yes, but I'm really just a singer-songwriter," I felt like I had painted myself into a corner with this years-long "accounting thing" that began with my very first job as a "fiscal officer" in 1975.

On Friday, January 12, 2007 after setting a personal New Year's resolution to be more focused on my singer-songwriter career, I received a call from an accounting temp agency that had my resume and wanted to place me in a temporary assignment for a couple weeks. A company's controller had suddenly resigned and they needed to have someone with experience to fill in until they could find a permanent replacement. I reluctantly agreed to start the following Monday and spent the entire weekend beating myself up over the decision, but I needed the money and didn't want to burn a bridge with the agency.

It had been awhile since I had the experience of starting a new job, and Monday, January 15, 2007 was a nerve-racking morning, but I found my way to the building where the company was located and entered the office. I met with the president for a few minutes as he filled me in on the company and what he believed needed to be accomplished for the week. He explained how the previous controller had resigned, left suddenly and so was no longer there to help out. We started to walk back to the office where the previous controller worked and when we came to the door, the nameplate on the door said "Mark H Nelson." It got me to wondering whatever happened to my old friend, Mark Nelson.

As we were going over some of Mark's work and getting on Mark's computer workstation with his old password, curiosity got the best of me, and I commented to the president that I used to know a "Mark H Nelson." The president casually said "Oh really, where was that?" I said "Bismarck, North Dakota." The president paused, and looked over at me with some wonderment, and said "Mark was previously from North Dakota." I said "are you serious…..did he have a strange looking eye?" (the Mark I know had a glass eye), the president said Mark did have a funny eye. It was almost as if the world as I knew it came to an end, could it be possible that in a small company in a place hundreds of miles away and across a span of 31 years that I could be replacing the very guy that hired me in my first accounting job????? Remember, Mark wasn't an accountant when I knew him, he didn't even have a high school diploma.

It WAS my old boss, Mark Nelson. I called him and we reconnected. As it turns out, he also got his MBA…at Vanderbilt, that's what brought him to Nashville. As for accounting, he said he really didn't see himself as an accountant either, he left to assume a job as a programmer and database developer. He asked me how my music career was going (he hadn't forgotten about that), and said he always knew I was destined to follow my singer-songwriter passion and that I wasn't really an accountant at heart.

I guess sometimes when you think you have life figured out, you get thrown a curve ball from somewhere on the other side of the universe…..or maybe it's just God's not so subtle way of reminding you to follow your calling and to make use of the gifts and talents he gave you.

Oh, by the way, did I ever mention that I am a singer-songwriter………

Chapter Twenty Two

Grandma Benson's Piano

An old piano graces the entrance to our home in Nashville. It is a Monarch upright grand piano made by Baldwin in Chicago, Illinois in 1924 and the serial number is 164239. It was purchased brand new by my grandmother, Alice Gausemel Benson, sometime between 1924 and when she married my grandfather, Stanley Benson, in 1926.

The piano began its life in a farmhouse about 15 miles south of Bowman, North Dakota where during its life there, brought much musical pleasure and provided a wonderful musical education for my mother and her three sisters. I'm sure that the piano provided the basis for the "Benson Sisters" learning to sing and made it possible for them to go out and share their singing talents at numerous events and gatherings. I don't remember much about my grandma's playing, but have certainly heard the family's recollections of their experiences.

The Benson family and the piano moved to Bowman in about 1940 to a small house, then to another small house, and eventually moved to the larger two story house that I remember when I was growing up. That's where I first encountered the piano. I took piano lessons for a while when I was six or seven years old and even though we had a piano out on the farm, I would play that piano when we visited grandma and grandpa. In 1969, they moved to smaller ranch style house across from the park in Bowman. The house had a first floor bedroom so grandma and grandpa could more easily get around.

My grandfather, Stanley, passed away in 1974 and when my grandmother, Alice, died in 1981, the sisters decided that the piano should go to my mother. But, my mother decided that she and dad didn't really have room for it and asked me if I would like to move it to our house in Dickinson, North Dakota where Sandy and I were living at the time and we agreed. Lawrence Stokes, the guy that my grandma originally purchased the piano from, was contacted to move it to our house at 1066 Dell Avenue in Dickinson. With a little effort, Lawrence got the piano down to the basement which was the only place we had room for it. I immediately got reacquainted with the piano and began relearning to play and to use it as an additional tool to write songs.

In 1983, the company I worked for, Rocky Mountain Geophysical, decided to relocate to Denver, Colorado and after much consideration, Sandy and I decided to move also. The company was providing a semi trailer to move us, so we loaded up the piano along with our household belongings and took it to Denver. Lawrence Stokes again toiled to bring that bulky piano up out of the basement and load it on that trailer. When we first arrived in Denver, our stuff was stored in a storage facility for two weeks until our house became available to occupy. We then rented a U-Haul truck to move all our belongings to our new house at 8727 East Girard Avenue in Denver. Being unsure where we wanted the piano to be placed, it remained in our garage for about a year where it would have been exposed to many variations in temperature.

One night we had a party at our house which was attended by some friends and mostly co-workers and owners from my company. After a considerable amount of alcohol was consumed, some of the guys decided to demonstrate their strength and masculinity by moving the piano into the house.

It still bears a few scars from that episode, but I was thankful it was finally available to for me to play again. I realized that it probably should be tuned so we contacted a piano tuner in 1985 (the piano would have been 64 years old). The piano tuner was amazed at how well the piano had retained its tuning and that it was in such good shape. My mom told me she couldn't ever remember it being tuned, although I'm sure it must have been. At this point, the piano had been moved six times.

I wrote some great songs on that piano in Denver including "In Your Eyes" for my first album and "The Prince" which I recently recorded for my newest album release in 2008. Denver was the place were our son Clark was born, and he started playing the piano in the first grade. He would come home from school and start playing melodies on the piano by ear that he remembered from music class. We then found a piano teacher for him.

As my musical destiny became more urgent, in 2002 we made the move to Nashville, Tennessee. Of course the piano came with us, we moved our stuff with a Mayflower moving van. The movers took good care of the piano and placed it in the entry by our front door where it remains today. After a couple years in Nashville, Clark resumed his piano lessons and has become a very good pianist. In early 2007, as Clark was playing often, I noticed that there were a few notes that were out of tune and I knew the piano should be tuned. We called a neighborhood acquaintance, Jim Kirby, to tune the piano. Jim was the piano player for Roy Orbison for the last 8 years of Roy's life and is an incredible player. Jim was also amazed at the condition of the piano and how well it had maintained its tuning (it was then 83 years old). He almost dropped over when I told him that it hadn't been tuned since 1985 (22 years and a move to Nashville). I'm now wondering if it is actually possible that this piano has only been tuned twice since it was purchased by my grandmother in the mid 1920's and moved seven times.

Clark has played a number of pianos in lessons and recitals, he takes lessons at Shuff's music in Franklin TN from Ken Rarick and the store is constantly rotating the pianos. Clark says that our piano is still his favorite and has the best touch of all the pianos he has played. I too have a renewed interest in this piano and am playing something almost every day. I am now convinced this piano carries a spirit with it and I want to use it on my next recording project, even though the sustain pedal is a little squeaky.

Recently, on a sunny spring morning as the rising sun streamed in the doorway on the piano, I felt the urge to just touch it, to lay my hands on the top of it. I was totally consumed by the memory impulses of my mom and my grandma and their musical history on this piano as well as the memories of my own experiences with it. The worn marks on the ivory and black keys brought back images of the fingers that made them. I was reminded of the stories I was told about the family's gathering around the piano and singing in the old days. I thought about how this piano has contributed to my son's musical ability and how he may touch others lives with his skills.

I am so thankful that my grandmother's legacy and her spirit continue to bless our family through this old Monarch Upright Grand. God willing, I will pass these blessings on down the line.

Chapter Twenty Three

A Story of Guitars and Spirits

From an early age, I was fascinated by guitars. In the sixth grade, my parents got me a Sears & Roebuck Silvertone guitar and signed me up for lessons with a local guitar teacher. My fascination soon turned to frustration as learning to play the guitar turned out to be more difficult than I anticipated. My hands and fingers were small and the Silvertone wasn't well suited for a beginner like me. After a few months, I quit taking guitar lessons. At the time, I thought I would soon resume lessons, but it would prove to be many years before I again picked up the guitar.

In my junior and senior years in high school, we started the band which would become *"Young Imagination"*, but we were a brass and rhythm band like Herb Alpert and the Tijuana Brass with me playing trumpet. We didn't have a guitar player. Eventually, it occurred to me that if I were to finally learn guitar, we could be a rock band! Now. I had a motivation to pick up that old Silvertone again and learn to play it, but I never did resume lessons. I bought a guitar book that focused on popular music and bar chords. My hands were still a little small (and still are today), but with a little work and practice, I could finally play the bar chords and play along with songs on records and radio. However, that old Silvertone wouldn't last long, I eventually got a used Fender electric guitar which proved to be much easier to play.

Throughout the *Young Imagination* days and my early college jazz band years, I played the Fender. I had gotten pretty attached to it and had personalized it with a red sticker that said "LOVE". One weekend while I was visiting my parents, I left the guitar in the music department equipment room at Dickinson State. When I returned and showed up for the next jazz band rehearsal, to my horror, my guitar was gone! It had been stolen over the weekend. For a while I borrowed a guitar to get by while I decided what type of guitar to buy to replace my stolen Fender. Sometimes even today, I wonder if I might someday see someone playing my old Fender guitar with that "LOVE" decal on it.

At this point in my life, I was being influenced by John Denver, Jim Croce and others who were playing acoustic guitars. I felt that if I had to buy a new guitar, I might as well shop for an acoustic model. I had noticed that Jim Croce & Glen Campbell were playing these new Ovation acoustic/electric guitars and thought that would make sense for me. I made a trip to Marguerite's Music in Jamestown, North Dakota where I knew and trusted the store salesman, Don, and he recommended a top of the line Ovation that looked perfect for me. The store had only one of this particular model and it was kind of expensive. I wandered around the store for awhile trying to justify spending the money. When I returned to the area to look at the guitar again, I found another person checking out the guitar. This wasn't just another guitar player, it was a guy I recognized from a well known Christian band that I had seen on TV! He told my friend Don, the salesman, that he was looking for this particular model and wanted to buy it! Just then, Don noticed me standing there and he told the guy that I had expressed interest in buying the guitar first. If my mind wasn't already made up, it certainly was then! I bought the Ovation. This Ovation has served me well and had been my primary guitar for over 20 years. Even today, when I pick it up, it feels like an old friend.

In 1997, I began playing writer's nights in Nashville and noticed that not many people played Ovation guitars, so I felt the need to acquire an all-wood guitar. After playing many different models in music stores, I settled on a Guild acoustic/electric F65ce that had a smaller neck. I thought the smaller neck would make the guitar easier on my small hands and make a better player out of me, and in addition, it was a very pretty guitar with a sunburst color. The Guild F65ce was a relatively rare model and always seemed to attract some attention. That was cool! But, as things sometimes go, the Guild never lived up to my expectations for feel and playability. It seemed like my fingers never felt right on the neck and eventually the neck began to have some alignment problems.

Before buying the Guild, I had purchased an inexpensive six string Seagull guitar to use around the house and it started to occur to me that the Seagull, made of cedar and mahogany, felt much better in my hands than the Guild. I also went back to my old trusty 1973 Ovation guitar to play live, since it was still my old friend. I had resolved to continue playing the Ovation live or to put a pickup on the Seagull and try it out on stage.

One warm late summer Friday evening in 2005, while I was relaxing on our deck and having a beer, our neighbor Jerry Taylor came over to visit. He was carrying a guitar case and he said he had purchased the guitar on Ebay and wondered if I would check it out. It was a Takamine NP15c which was manufactured about 1995. It had a cedar top and mahogany back and sides similar to my Seagull, but was a much more of a top of the line guitar. From the moment my hands touched that guitar, I knew it was special. I picked it up and strummed a few chords and the guitar seemed to resonate through my body and soul like no other guitar I had ever played. I never before thought I could like a Takamine, but I knew I had to have this one.

Jerry must have sensed that I connected to the guitar and he offered to let me try it out for a while. He had collected other guitars, so it wasn't critical that he play this one. The following Sunday, I was scheduled to play in church so I used the Takamine, and a few days later I played at a writer's night. I was total consumed by it. Jerry told me that if I really wanted this Takamine, he would sell it to me for $500, which was a reasonable price. A few weeks later, I went to a guitar shop downtown and sold the Guild F65ce for $460 and finally bought the Takamine from Jerry.

I don't have an explanation, but somehow this Takamine has a spirit that has connected with me. From the depths of time and space, this guitar and I were meant to be joined. I sometimes wonder where it came from before Jerry, who owned it and who played it. What is its history? Am I being influenced by the souls of others? My destiny has likely been altered by this guitar, it has been a big inspirational factor in my songs and performances since I have acquired it. I know I am and can be a better performer and songwriter because I have known this guitar.

Will this Takamine be the last guitar I will ever play or own? Probably not, but my singer-songwriter career is better because of it. Come to think of it, my Ovation always seemed to have a special spirit also. Ironically, the manufacturer Kaman makes both Ovation and Takamine.

Chapter Twenty Four

Of Buzzards And Hugh Bennett

On my morning walk in the summer of 2006 as I was approaching the corner of Woodhurst and San Marcos near our Nashville home, I saw four huge winged, strange looking creatures in yard of the house on the corner. At first I thought they might be wild turkeys, but as I approached, I realized they were buzzards feasting on a dead animal in the yard. In all my years of living previously in North Dakota and Colorado, and to that point in Tennessee, I had never seen a buzzard.

On my way back to the house, I saw a guy who I would see quite often, who frequently walked his dog in our neighborhood, however, we had never formally introduced ourselves. I could hardly contain my surprise of just encountering buzzards in our neighborhood! As the guy approached, I told him about the buzzards and that it was the first time I had ever seen a buzzard. He informed me that it was a relatively common occurrence and asked me where I was from that I would not have ever seen a buzzard. I mentioned I was originally from North Dakota. He said "I used to do some production work for Lawrence Welk who was from North Dakota." Of course, I knew that Lawrence Welk was from North Dakota and was an entertainer, so I figured this guy was in the music business somehow.

He was wearing a polo shirt that had "Hugh Bennett Productions" stitched over the pocket, so I said "your name must be Hugh Bennett." He said that indeed it was. I was curious about his background and asked more about he and his company and was amazed to learn that he was involved with quite a few major productions that involved sound and video. He was actually very well known to the Nashville music community even though I couldn't remember hearing of him.

Hugh went on to tell me that he was the one that actually started songwriter nights in Nashville way back in the 1970's at the Exit Inn. I had always thought that songwriter nights were started at the Bluebird Café in the 1980's, so when I got home, I checked on the internet, and he was in fact credited with starting writer's nights in Nashville.

Hugh and I had a great conversation, we had something in common because I had started the first continuous songwriter show in Denver. Hugh is a great supporter of singer-songwriters and has known most of the best. He said he still gets Christmas cards from Kris Kristofferson.

Like many music business folks, Hugh had his past share of experiences and a self imposed hard life from substance abuse. I learned from our conversation that Hugh had Hepatitis C and was fighting for his survival from the disease. I could relate to this because my brother Scott had Hepatitis C and ultimately died from the disease in 1995. For all that he was going through, Hugh had an amazingly positive attitude about life. He always appeared happy and was a fun guy to be around.

Hugh definitely had stories to tell! He had been a road manager for Johnny Paycheck among others and with this and all of the other functions Hugh performed in the music business, he could weave an unbelievable string of tales. Not only were our conversations enjoyable, but were a learning experience about music people and life in general.

Hugh has moved out of our neighborhood, so I don't get to see him much these days. I still consider him a member of my "informal advisory committee" and know I can turn to him for advice and inspiration. Hugh's life has been full of risks and challenges, disappointments and triumphs, and as such, is a perfect example of the celebration of life. The world is a better place and I am better person for the blessing of knowing Hugh.

And to think this all came about because of buzzards! The moral of this story might be if the buzzards are circling and ready to close in on me, I need to remember Hugh Bennett.

THE MOUNTAIN - *A Poem*

(narrated on the CD *"Life Is Good"*)

I made my way up the mountain
Through the rugged valleys
Against the rushing rivers
And over the jagged rocks………

When I got high enough……
I turned….and I looked back down
At the lush and green and fertile plain….
That I was struggling to get away from

I wondered why……
Is the the grass really greener somewhere?

But, I continued to climb… against the driven snow,
The wind……. and against the loneliness……
All in anticipation…… of what was on the other side

I finally got high enough
To peer beyond the top of the mountain
And I saw barren desert………….

And I knew it was time……
To turn and go back down……

But, in all of my sorrow and frustration from the climb,
I knew all was not lost……

For it was a mountain that had to be climbed

****

And with that said, life goes on and *Life Is Good!*

Continuing The Journey

My dream, is that my greatest stories have yet to be lived and written, and that those are stories where I have been able to make a difference in the world by passing on the experience and gifts I have received and the instincts I have acquired. I want to include some mentions here about others who have touched me in one way or another.

Jimmy Webb performed in concert at Dickinson State in the fall of 1971. I had the opportunity to meet Jimmy earlier in the day while they were wandering around campus, which made the upcoming show more real to me. At the show, when he introduced and told the story about the song "Galveston," it brought me the first realization of songs and stories going hand in hand. I was very familiar with Glen Campbell's hit version of the song, but Jimmy shed a whole new light on it…it was his song…a song about real life…it touched me because it came from his soul. Now, I strive to achieve that standard, I believe it is the essence of what singer-songwriters are meant to do.

Gary Puckett was a favorite of mine in the 60's and I attended his concert in Spearfish, South Dakota in 1970. We got to the show early and were able to wander backstage at the auditorium where Gary had just finished a sound check. He walked over and introduced himself to me and was the first entertainer I had ever met. He inquired about where I was from, and I said "a little town" in North Dakota. He said "what town?" and I responded "Scranton, but I'm sure you've never heard of it." He was from Minnesota and told me that he had been down US Highway 12 many times, which runs by

Scranton. It was lesson that these entertainers, who are household names, are real people and travel the same roads, literally and figuratively, that we do. Ironically, in 2002 in Nashville, I met and became friends with Kerry Chater, one of Gary's band mates from *Gary Puckett And The Union Gap*.

Greg Nelson, the now famous Christian producer for Sandi Patti and others, produced my first recordings in Bismarck, North Dakota. Greg believed in me and treated me with respect. He lives in Nashville, and I reconnected with him in the late 90's, after not seeing him for over 20 years. As we know, it is a small world, Rollie Mains, who was Sandi Patti's keyboard player for many years, became our choir director at church, and played keyboard and strings on my *Life Is Good* album. When I first met Greg Nelson in Bismarck, he was working with Tom Netherton to help get a deal with Lawrence Welk, and coincidentally, our new choir director, Ted Wilson, who replaced Rollie, saws his wife previously dated Tom Netherton.

Ray Griff, a well known singer and songwriter in Nashville in the 70's, was a judge at the Country Jamboree at Dickinson State in 1975 where I was a male vocalist winner doing original songs. Ray made a point to come back stage to meet me, and tell me he voted for me. What a confidence builder that gesture was for me!

Bobby Vee, the popular singer from the early 60's, is from North Dakota. As a result of my song "Dakota, I've Not Forgotten" being chosen to represent the North Dakota Centennial in 1989, I was fortunate to have the opportunity to open the North Dakota Centennial Show which was headlined by Bobby and Roy Clark. I met Bobby then, but we again crossed paths many years later in Bowman, North Dakota at their county fair, where Bobby was headlining. We had a good conversation in his van backstage where I learned more of his history. It was interesting to learn from Bob Dylan's book, that Bob was a big fan of Bobby Vee before Bob became famous.

The Beatles....what can I say? I saw them on Ed Sullivan in February, 1964. We all wanted to be like them.

It is helpful to reflect on these encounters and be thankful. It is also humbling and gives me a sense of responsibility to touch others as I have been touched.

Where does my journey go from here? I keep writing, songs and stories, and plan to share them. I look forward to another album project, inspirational based, to be released in 2009 or 2010. I am developing a TV show for a cable channel, that will bring to life, the stories and songs along this spiritual road I am on. As host of the show, I plan to feature, and be an advocate for, the things in my life that have mattered most.....growing up on the farm, the musical education, the small town churches and communities, and independent singer-songwriters. I want to promote the "coolness factor" of music education at an early age, and encourage more people to become music teachers. I want to leave a legacy for the future of the music industry, and for our youth of tomorrow.

In this day and age, it should come as no surprise, you can find me. I am on Facebook, MySpace, and Twitter, as well as others. My music is on iTunes, Rhapsody, and all other notable digital sites.

I'm heading out on the road again, to write another song, to climb another mountain, to create more *Tales From A Singer-Songwriter*. I hope you will be blessed, and be inspired, on your own spiritual road.

www.ingramcontent.com/pod-product-compliance
Lightning Source LLC
Chambersburg PA
CBHW031652040426

42453CB00006B/282